You're a Teacher…So Act Like One!

You're a Teacher…So Act Like One!

♦

Improving Your "Stage Presence" in the Classroom

Daniel Tricarico

Writers Club Press

San Jose New York Lincoln Shanghai

You're a Teacher...So Act Like One!
Improving Your "Stage Presence" in the Classroom

Writers Club Press
an imprint of iUniverse, Inc.

For information address:
iUniverse, Inc.
5220 S. 16th St., Suite 200
Lincoln, NE 68512
www.iuniverse.com

ISBN: 0-595-23402-X

Printed in the United States of America

To Michael and Janet Tricarico

Contents

ACKNOWLEDGMENTS

I would like to thank the following people, many of whom were the teachers who taught me to act, write, or teach: Kay Adams, Kristin Amundson, Geoffrey Anderson, Susan Arthur, Danelle Barton, Clifford Bee, Cece Boehme-DeCew, Tedd Brent, Kerry Daggett, Katherine Faulconer, Laurey Sledd-Fontaine, Don and Rita Fields, Anne Foster, Suzanne Geba, Martin Gerrish, Ellen Gilmore, John Goodman, Michelle Granfield, John Holler, Edward Hollingsworth, Lucinda Holshue, Robin Luby, Leone McCoy, Chris Morrissey, Jane Schaffer, Audrey Seidel, and Mark Steckbauer. I would also like to thank Marlon Brando, Al Pacino, Robert DeNiro, Tom Hanks, Dustin Hoffman, Raymond Carver, and David Mamet for models that were such fun to aspire to.

And a special thank you to my wife, Valerie, and my daughters, Tatum and Tessa. Thanks for all your love, patience, and support.

INTRODUCTION

○ ○
"The habit of being daily on the stage and in the right
creative state is what produces actors who are masters of their
art."

—*Constantin Stanislavski*
An Actor Prepares

We have all witnessed certain acting performances, whether on-stage or
on film, which were so moving and powerful we left the playhouse or
movie theater feeling we had met a living, breathing human being. We
felt we had gained some insight into human nature. Some actor or
actress delved into a character's heart and soul and, through the use of
performance techniques, communicated to us the nuances of that character's joys, sorrows, dreams, hopes, and fears. The performer awakened our senses, captivated our attention, and touched our emotions.
In short, it was impossible for us to take our eyes from the performer
while he worked his magic.

Wouldn't it be wonderful if students had the same reaction to a
teacher when they left the classroom each day? Or even for one day, for
that matter.

It has been said that, as teachers, we perform in front of a live audience for five periods every day of the week. The metaphor is apt. We
are on the boards more times a week than an actor in a Broadway
show. And yet, teachers are never taught the importance of performance techniques—projection, energy, inflection, pacing, timing—which allow those Broadway thespians to awe their audiences

1

night after night. Teachers might do well, then, to develop the kind of training in performance style and "stage presence" available to actors. What if our teachers, for example, had had the intensity of Robert DeNiro, the versatility of Meryl Streep, or simply the energy of a Robin Williams? How different would our educations have been? How much might we have learned?

Acting is about the communication of behavior and emotions. Teaching is about the communication of ideas and information. As educators, we have an opportunity to synergize our teaching styles by blending the two ends of the spectrum and providing our students with the full range of experience: attitude...emotion...information...ideas.

What a powerful approach to the classroom.

In this book, you will discover the skills which make that synergy possible.

Good teachers, of course, intuitively understand how a strong performance style makes for more engaging, entertaining, and powerful teaching. Not every teacher, though, understands how important it is to communicate with the audience. We all remember those teachers, who, day after dreadful day, bored us to death. Maybe their voices were flat or monotonous, or their delivery was poor and unfocused, or their pacing was funereal, or their lesson plans lacked the spark, variety, and depth that would have made learning an exciting and unpredictable adventure. Ask yourself: how much better would these teachers have been had they employed even the *simplest* of performance techniques?

My years of experience with acting and teaching have shown me the benefits of using performance techniques in the classroom. Sadly, teacher education programs do not address the issue of performance techniques or "stage presence" while they are training educators.

Teachers will find performance skills in this book they can integrate into their own personal teaching style and use to improve their presence in the classroom. They will learn how to use performance-oriented concepts such as costumes, props, music, and lighting in the classroom to not only increase the sense of drama and wonder in their lesson plans, but also in their students' lives. They will also discover other concepts actors use to ensure an optimum performance—relaxation, energy, action, environment, voice, pacing, mood, attitude, structure, and suspense. These elements of performance, which actors rely on everyday in every rehearsal and performance, also happen to be critical concepts for an effective teaching style.

While teaching is certainly not merely a matter of "entertaining" one's students, teachers must acknowledge that great performances they've seen have changed their perspectives and altered their windows to the world.

Wouldn't it be wonderful to do that for our students?

At this writing, I have been a public high school English teacher for fifteen years, and so the examples I give and the stories I tell will, for the most part, reflect that experience. The benefits I have seen using performance techniques in the classroom to help students read, understand, analyze, and enjoy literature are without number. Still, the concepts described in this book are just as useful to the elementary, middle, or junior high school teacher or the instructor who teaches a subject other than literature. Furthermore, these concepts, while pulled from many years of acting training, are geared for the classroom and have been modified for use by teachers.

Lastly, it is certainly my wish that this book is entertaining to read, but its primary purpose is as a reference. I envision you pulling it off the shelf, rereading a passage on whatever technique you are hoping to practice, and coming away with an exercise, an activity, or—at the very least—an insight. These precepts, however, work best not when used individually, but when blended seamlessly together. This takes practice. Good performance technique relies on the integrated use of many skills, all working together to create a unique, original, and individual performance every hour we are in our classrooms.

Make a proactive choice to implement some or all of the performance techniques in the book. Give a good performance in your classroom. Remember the kind of teacher you wish your teachers had been or the teacher who *did* touch you with her enthusiasm and exuberance.

Be that teacher for your students.

PREPARATION

1

CONFIDENCE

"I have discovered The Secret of Life," said my 17 year-old niece who was visiting us recently.

"What's that, Stacey?" I asked.

"The Secret of Life," she said, clearly relishing her moment of drama, "is Confidence."

"Very good," I said. "You're probably right."

"And the secret to gaining confidence," she continued, "is to *act* like you have confidence."

Her satisfied smile indicated that she'd said her piece and was done.

Stacey's final comment, however, touched a nerve. I, too, had been working on my sense of confidence since I was her age—with only minor victories. I never seemed to have enough confidence and felt my lack of it was holding me back from greater success and accomplishment. As a younger man, I came to a similar conclusion as Stacey in regard to "acting" as if one had confidence, but whenever I tried this, it felt artificial and insincere—as if I were somehow betraying my true feelings and not being completely genuine with those around me.

Stacey's stellar accomplishments (valedictorian, 4.5 GPA in advanced classes, varsity athlete, editor-in-chief of her high school newspaper, softball scholarship offers to a number of universities) forced me to reconsider my perspective on *acting* confident. Clearly, it worked. And if anyone could act as if he had confidence, I reasoned, it should be I, having studied acting for more than a decade. Still, I continued to struggle with the issue of self-confidence in every area of my life. Stacey's declaration, however, renewed my faith that each of us can develop the self-confidence we need to succeed in life.

Confidence, at its heart, is the personal belief in one's own abilities. It is the security of knowing that in doing your best, you will most likely accomplish your goals. In a sense, then, confidence is The Absence of Doubt.

Lack of confidence—or The *Presence* of Doubt—forces us to question our abilities. It causes us to have generalized fear regarding our performance: What if I'm not a good teacher? What if I don't know my subject area well enough? Even while fighting this lack of confidence, we can sometimes experience even more specific doubts and anxieties: What if I can't come up with exciting, meaningful assignments for my students? we think, or: What if I'm shortchanging, or even missing, some valuable concept in my lesson or unit? This second-guessing can be detrimental not only to one's teaching style, but to the general "stage presence" of the teacher as well.

These doubts can paralyze our attempts to perform as educators and cause us to spend much of our professional time and energy questioning our techniques, ability, and skill. With a little confidence, though, this time and energy could be much better spent improving what is already powerful about what we do.

Here are four easy methods for creating personal confidence:

Creating Confidence Through Imitation

One beginning method for improving confidence is to imitate the self-assured style of an effective role model. As teachers know, imitation is an excellent technique for learning new concepts. Imitating an expert allows a student an opportunity to "try on" particular skills (anything from cooking to archery to taking blood) before making those skills his own. Mimicking a role model is hardly a revolutionary idea. Athletes do it. Writers do it. Actors do it. Every teenager who has picked out the opening notes to "Stairway to Heaven" on a cheap six-string guitar has done it.

For me, it was Perry. I watched Perry during our junior high school dances. Just from spying on him out of the corner of my eye while on the dance floor, he taught me (without realizing it himself) to master the in-the-air scissors kick, the 360 degree turn, and the slyest way to inch closer to a girl during a slow dance. Critical skills, naturally, for a thirteen year-old to master. By imitating the expert moves of this eighth-grade John Travolta, I learned to increase my confidence in my own fancy footwork on the dance floor.

For teachers, this brand of imitation as a learning process is an amazingly simple activity. Most likely, the "expert" is just down the hall. Seek out a veteran teacher whose teaching style, confidence, and ability you admire. You may already have someone in mind; someone who has always struck you as relaxed, confident, and in control. Arrange to observe that teacher for a lesson or two. As you observe, take notes on that teacher's individual presentation style. Document the teacher's behavior, posture, movement, actions, and dialogue with students. What is it about that teacher's style that appears so confident and self-assured?

The confident stance?

The seemingly spontaneous jokes?

The strong knowledge of the subject matter?

The highly organized lesson plan?

The neat, in-depth, and clearly explained handouts and worksheets?

The neat and orderly room environment?

The plentiful materials, supplies, and props?

The intensive preparation?

After returning to your own classroom and reviewing your notes, begin to shamelessly sift those aspects of your role model's teaching style that you admired into your own personal repertoire. Not only won't that teacher mind, but he or she will most likely be quite flattered! Don't worry, though, if at first not everything feels completely "right" or "comfortable." That's okay. It will take awhile for you to put your own mark on things. The key is to notice what works for *you*. If you visited a certain teacher, for example, because you admired his vocal delivery, or for his discipline procedures, that doesn't mean that you will be copying the physical layout of his room.

Visit another teacher for that!

By analyzing what makes these other teachers appears confident (and remember, as my niece said, that sometimes it is only the *appearance* of confidence), you will make great strides in improving your own self-assurance. Soon you will feel more organized, accomplished, and in control. This new sense of confidence will also make you more relaxed which, in turn, will cause you to enjoy what you're doing even more. As the beginning writer's first stories might emulate Hemingway's minimalist sentence structure, the new painter Van Gogh's brush strokes, or even the novice diver Louganis's half-gainers, you, too, will incorporate into your own work certain elements you observed in your role model's style. And like the Little Leaguer who copies Barry Bond's batting stance, what you copy from your role model will eventually become so seamlessly absorbed into your own unique style that it will evolve into an integral component of your own arsenal of teaching methods. Before long, your level of confidence will increase, and it will be impossible to tell where your relaxed and assured style begins and your role model's ends.

Creating Confidence Through Personal Achievement

Another method for improving confidence is to take the necessary steps to reach your goals. Any motivational speaker will tell us that to reach our potential as individuals, we must learn to believe in ourselves and our abilities. It is through this confidence, the rich and powerful know, that we develop our aspirations and then meet them. As my niece so astutely pointed out, sometimes learning to believe in ourselves involves behaving as if we already do.

A college teacher I once had explained this concept another way. He drew three columns across the chalkboard and labeled them with the words HAVE/DO/BE. He said this was a paradigm for personal achievement. He also said that, as a continuum, you could start at either end, or even in the middle if you wanted. For example, if we wanted to BE a certain thing, we should have what we needed to BE that thing, and do what we needed to do to BE that thing, and the odds that we would ultimately BE that thing would increase dramatically.

Similarly, if we wanted to HAVE something, we should be what we needed to be to HAVE it, do what we needed to do to HAVE it, and our odds of HAVING that very thing would radically improve. I suppose if we wanted to DO something in particular we might work from the middle outward on the spectrum.

HAVE	DO	BE
What materials, supplies, experience, etc. do I need to HAVE to reach my goals?	What do I need to DO to reach my goals? (i.e. what actions should I take?)	What do I have to BE in order to reach my goals?

Here's a practical example of the HAVE/DO/BE philosophy in action:

If I wanted to BE a skydiver, for instance, then I should HAVE the equipment and training a skydiver HAS and DO the things a skydiver DOES (like packing my own chute and practicing my landings). I still may never hurl myself from an airplane into the wild blue yonder, but I will have significantly increased my chances that this event might someday take place (and I will be more prepared if it does). I will have created for myself a situation and environment where I am more likely to reach my dreams.

The continuum works the other way as well. If I want to HAVE a yacht, I should BE a more committed, dedicated, and focused worker, DO the work and take the steps necessary to get those promotions or make those big sales, and then I greatly increase my chances of increasing my income to the point where I can purchase my yacht. And life being how it is, if I'm only ever able to manage a little Hobie sailboat, at least I had a dream!

The irony is that not only will I come closer to achieving my goals, but in the preparation and practice I get pursuing them—and in the practice of the HAVE/DO/BE continuum—I will most likely increase my confidence that I *can* achieve them, that I *will* achieve them, and that I *deserve* the benefits associated *with* achieving them.

Here are two HAVE/DO/BE examples for the classroom:

* If I want to BE a teacher whose classroom is perceived as a warm, inviting, and fun place to learn, then I should:
* HAVE lots of projects and posters on the walls and other "comforting" objects around the room. For this to happen, I should:
* DO the projects as classwork and have my students make posters to hang or bring in other fun objects to share and dress up the room.

* If I want to BE more knowledgeable about my subject matter and be perceived as an expert in my field, then I should:
* HAVE an advanced degree (Master's or Doctorate) in my area of expertise. For this to happen, I should:
* DO (complete) the legwork necessary to apply to my local university and complete the classes that will allow me to earn that Master's or Doctorate.

These may seem like simple steps, but sometimes lack of confidence (that pesky Presence of Doubt) so clouds our intentions, our desires, and our motivation, that many times we are unsure of where to begin in an effort to achieve our goals, and so end up languishing in the same old routines in which we've always been.

Following the HAVE/DO/BE continuum is a powerful avenue toward personal success and increased confidence because it improves our personal achievement which increases our self-assurance and self-esteem. If you want to increase your confidence in yourself and your abilities, set a reasonable, but challenging goal, then achieve it (At first, make those goals small ones: cleaning your house or car more often, working on a better vocabulary, taking that Tai Chi class, writing more letters to friends, etc.)

Creating Confidence Through Behavior

Doug, an old friend of mine, had an uncanny knack of looking like he belonged wherever he was, even if he didn't. While still in high school, he discovered this talent and was able to cut class by acting as if he was on his way somewhere else. His purposeful walk, sense of important mission, and relaxed demeanor kept him out of trouble, as he *appeared* as if he was doing exactly what he was supposed to be doing and not, in fact, ditching History or Geometry.

Amazingly, he was once able to "act" his way into the Academy Awards in Los Angeles. I was sitting at home that night, like two billion others, watching the Oscars from the comfort of my living room. They were introducing each of the stars over the opening credits as they usually do, and I was just settling in. I almost choked on my popcorn when I saw Doug standing behind Clint Eastwood, looking as casual and nonchalant as if he were relaxing in his own backyard. He would later tell me that he was able to witness the entire award show from the inside, after confidently breezing into the auditorium through a side door, just by behaving as if he was on his way somewhere important, as if he "belonged" exactly where he was and had to get where he was going. This self-assured behavior encouraged others to have the same kind of confidence in his abilities that he had himself (even if that "ability" was to gain access to places where he didn't belong!).

Teachers can also alter their behavior in a way that projects a calm, relaxed, and self-assured persona. Learning to behave confidently is like trying on a new sweater that has a more "loud" or expressive color or pattern than you are used to wearing. At first it may seem too big or loose or scratchy, but the more you wear it, the more you start to see yourself as more naturally wearing those new colors or patterns, and the more likely someone will feel compelled to remark, "Oh, that new sweater is *you*!"

Similarly, even if you don't necessarily feel genuinely confident at first, practicing the behavior will allow your mind and body to develop a "memory" about how it "feels" to behave confidently which, in turn, will allow you to express that confidence more naturally and sincerely once you have gotten the "feel" of those new "colors." Then you will no longer be *acting* as if you have confidence, but will truly be feeling a fresh and invigorating sense of assurance in your teaching skills and style.

Confidence can be a tremendous asset in the classroom. Chances are, it is those teachers who exude a positive, self-assured, in control, and relaxed vibration as they teach who are usually perceived as stronger and more successful by students and colleagues alike.

Creating Confidence Through Preparation

A final confidence-builder teachers can borrow from the world of acting is the concept of preparation. Preparation is sacred in the world of acting. A serious actor would rather commit *hari kari* than walk on stage without having done the homework of knowing his lines, knowing the blocking (his specific movements on stage), or knowing who his character is inside and out. To attempt a performance without such preparation is, in short, professional suicide.

Teachers should feel the same way. They should know what the lesson plan is, what objectives they wish to meet, and what skills the students should know—every time they step on stage.

Preparation will not only serve you well on those days when the lesson is going smoothly, but will come in particularly handy on those days when it isn't. Much like performing, sometimes a day in the classroom provides us with mistakes, unplanned contingencies, or just plain accidents that we have to deal with. Preparation allows us to move through these times gracefully and with aplomb.

If a teacher is prepared, accidents will become only minor road bumps on the road to learning. An old trick of acting that picks up where preparation leaves off is this: Always act as if whatever is going on in the lesson is exactly what you meant to happen—even if it isn't. *Especially if it isn't.* Naturally, if the VCR suddenly eats your videotape and you have no backup plan, it's difficult to convince your students that that's exactly what you had planned. However, if you find you have an extra ten minutes at the end of class that you weren't expecting, and you have prepared enough to have a number of small activities to pull from in just such an emergency, it is critical to slide right into one without blinking. The transition into this new activity—one that you were not planning—is the behavior of a confident, self-assured teacher. Remember, only you as the teacher have seen the script. Your audience thinks the show is supposed to be going exactly as you lead them to believe.

I am certainly not advocating keeping the truth from our students, but imagine what a disaster it would be if an actor made a mistake on stage and suddenly broke character, stopped the action, turned the audience and said, "I'm sorry. I goofed. Can we try that last scene again? I wasn't quite prepared and forgot the line about the talcum powder..."

Confidence is a gift, but it is also a skill. We can be born with an aptitude toward it, or we can learn certain techniques to enhance the confidence we already possess. For teachers, the idea of confidence is best described as a Lack of Doubt. Preparation is always the best road to confidence and it will not only improve your confidence in yourself, but your students' confidence in their teacher as well.

Try this "simple" two step exercise in confidence:

1) Believe in yourself.
2) Believe in what you're doing.

2

RELAXATION AND BREATHING

An actor depends on a state of relaxation for an optimum performance. This is not, however, the kind of relaxation you feel while drifting off to sleep in a LA-Z-Boy recliner in front of the movie-of-the week, a bag of Lay's potato chips in your lap. An actor relies on his senses being in a state of readiness, of calmness, of poised anticipation of the performance ahead. To ensure that his skills are at their peak before going on stage, the actor has prepared, warmed-up, and taken a moment to center his mind, focus his attentions, and concentrate his energies on the performance at hand. A serious actor spends hours in training, hours in practice, and hours in perfecting a truckload of techniques that will relax his mind, body, and spirit.

For a teacher to teach effectively, he must also be relaxed. This is true whether or not the day's lesson has anything to do with performing. To execute any job successfully, it is necessary to minimize stress, tension, and anxiety. Tension and anxiety, especially, are the enemy of a good performance and can kill an otherwise brilliant lesson. Tension suffocates the ability to communicate the subject matter clearly and effectively, while anxiety clouds a teacher's purpose and blurs his priorities.

No matter how inspired and thoughtful the message, if a teacher experiences tension either in his mind, body, or voice, the students will not receive the message as clearly as possible. Relaxation is the first step to performing effectively as a teacher. And the first step in relaxation is gaining control of the breath.

Breathing is our lifeforce. It guides the rhythm of our being. If we are breathing rapidly, the pace of our life can't help but be swift, active, and—in many cases—filled with the adrenaline rush of a busy schedule or active lifestyle. Conversely, if our breathing is deep, slow, and measured, the pace of our lives will tend to be slower, more mellow, and less impulsive. Neither is better or worse, however. There are times when we should move, think, and act quickly and with purpose. Other times, though, we should be reflective, thoughtful, and cautious. Our breath cannot only be a signal as to what pace were are keeping, but to what pace will suit us best for the task at hand. With the proper control, we can adjust our breathing to fit our pace if that's what's necessary; or, we can use our current pace as a guide toward the direction in which to guide the rhythm of our breathing.

To understand what I mean by gaining control of the breath impulse, try this: The next time it's been a crazy day in the classroom and you are feeling unusually harried, pressured, or stressed, take a moment and just stop (for those of you already saying, "If I could take a moment to stop I wouldn't be feeling harried, pressured, or stressed," I truly mean it will only take a few minutes; and it can make the difference as to how you'll feel for the rest of the day—inside and outside of the classroom). If you can turn out some or all of the lights in the classroom, do so. Close your eyes. Sit in a straight-backed chair. Make sure you have excellent posture. Keep your back and neck straight and aligned. Next, clear your mind (Easier said than done, I know, but everything you are worried about will still be there when this exercise is done, so you might as well give the process a whirl). Now, visualize a pleasant setting: a beach, a park, your living room with the fireplace roaring, whatever works for you. Then slowly begin listening to your own breathing. This is your internal rhythm. Your Personal Force. No one else has one like it. Own it. Listen to how fast or slow it is. How deep or shallow. Whether you breathe through your nose or mouth or both.

Once you've been introduced to your internal breath impulse, begin to slow the breathing. Do not make any other adjustment until you feel the impulse to breathe again, then make the breath deeper, slower, and more measured. Keep your mind on that pleasant scene you've created. Keep your posture straight in the chair. Once you've slowed your breath to a relaxing rhythm keep that pace steadily for at least a minute or two. Keep your eyes closed while you are breathing. As you practice, it will become easier to access your internal breath rhythm and reach this relaxed state more quickly each time. But it takes total commitment. The irony is that though this exercise cannot be rushed, if it is taken seriously it moves very quickly.

Your breathing will eventually slow to the point where your body follows suit and relaxes. At this point, slowly open your eyes. Rise slowly and turn on the lights. You should feel less harried and less stressed. For the first few times you practice accessing your breathing rhythm, it may be in your best interest to practice somewhere you can work relaxed and uninterrupted, like your own home. Eventually, the process will be familiar enough to you that even a few minutes in a typically chaotic school or classroom environment, and you'll feel more relaxed and in tune with your own body, breath, and relaxation impulse. It takes time and practice to perfect a skill like this, especially if you are not used to listening to signals from your own body, so don't give up if you don't see immediate results.

Keep trying.

The entire process described above should take about five minutes. No matter how busy a school gets, every teacher can carve out five minutes. If you are an elementary school teacher, do it while the little ones are at recess. If you are a secondary teacher, lock your door during the passing period and don't let the students in until you have control of your breath. This will then give you more control over the class when they *do* come in.

The key to relaxation in our performances begins with every breath we take, every day. Doesn't a nice relaxed classroom setting feel wonderful? If it does, start breathing. Give yourself that sense of poised anticipation. Place yourself in control of your own performance through the elimination of tension, stress, and anxiety. Relaxing your mind, body, and spirit will improve your performance skill and your success in the classroom.

I guarantee it.

3

MEDITATION

Whenever anyone says the word "meditation," the first picture that jumps to mind is of The Beatles sitting cross-legged on the floor in front of the long-haired, bearded Maharishi Mahesh Yogi, listening intently as the guru pontificated about visualizations, chants, and mantras. This mental image I have may or may not have ever really happened, but the first time I heard the word, it was in relation to The Fab Four and their experiences with the Maharishi, so somehow the image stuck in my mind. Later in the 70's, I would watch this man who created (or at least promoted) Transcendental Meditation (known worldwide as simply, "TM") on *The Merv Griffin Show,* and I was struck by how peaceful and serene a being he was. Even at six or seven years of age, I understood that it had something to do with this thing called "meditation." As a result, I have been a fan of the idea of meditation, although not always its most dedicated practitioner, for most of my life. The Maharishi's type of meditation, however, is not exactly the kind I will be talking about in this chapter.

According to the *Oxford American Dictionary,* the definition of the word, "meditation," is "to think deeply, to contemplate," or, "to plan in one's mind." The form of meditation suggested by that definition is extremely helpful to educators. It can clear the mind, focus the purpose, and increase our energy. It can also be of tremendous use to a teacher who wishes to hone his or her performing instincts.

I have gone back to various forms of meditation throughout my life. I performed in my first high school play as a junior in 1979. I didn't come on until the second act. It was always very quiet backstage. Half way through the first act, I found a corner in the wings next to the sound equipment. It was a perfect spot because no one was talking, and I could only barely hear the actors on stage. I sat cross-legged on the floor (imitating the funky lotus positions of my heroes The Beatles, no doubt), closed my eyes, and concentrated on my breath. I certainly had no formal training in any serious form of meditation and yet, for several minutes, I attempted to clear my mind and relax my body through sheer force and desire. It was an elementary form of meditation, to say the least, but I feel certain—even today—that my performances in that play benefited from those few minutes of silence and concentration. This approach to meditation still helps me relax and focus my attention and energies today as I attempt to perfect my performing skills as a teacher.

Meditation is essentially a concentration exercise. According *to The Relaxation Stress Reduction Workbook*, meditation is, "the practice of attempting to focus your attention on one thing at a time." Not exactly a popular perspective in modern America, is it? We are much more content if we can be cooking spaghetti, diapering a baby, talking on the cell phone, watching television, and playing the lottery all at the same time.

Then, of course, we are being "productive citizens."

Teachers are the same way. Many feel they are not effective unless they are doing a million things at once: answering questions, hole-punching papers, correcting quizzes, ordering supplies, handing out bathroom passes, etc. What meditation attempts to do is allow you the luxury of focusing on one thing at a time so that you do it both quickly and accurately.

The Relaxation and Stress Reduction Workbook talks about two kinds of meditation: mantra and gazing. Mantra, or fixed meditation, involves closed eyes and repeating (or "chanting," if you prefer) a word or series of words while focusing your mind on your breath. Essentially chanting the word just creates a constant rhythm that you can focus on and this helps eliminate all the other static and distraction in your mind. A gazing meditation, on the other hand, involves choosing a fixed object in the room to focus on (candle flame, flower, smudge of dirt on the wall), and your concentration on the object—known in LaMaze circles as your focal point—also helps eliminate distraction while you clear your mind.

During our first pregnancy, for example, my wife and I had practiced gazing meditation, and a friend loaned us a little stuffed Eeyore doll to use as the focal point. Through a serious of family visits, room changes, and snack times, my wife's focal point during the actual labor ended up being a crumpled and greasy bag of stale Winchell's donuts. Clearly, then, what the object is really doesn't matter as long as you have *something* to focus on.

In both cases, mantra or gazing, the process is simple. Start by getting in touch with your breath impulse (see last chapter). Choose either a mantra or gazing meditation. While breathing deeply and smoothly in your own natural rhythm, clear your mind of thoughts and begin your mantra or focus on your fixed object. Breath naturally while focusing on the sound of the mantra or the visual image of the object you've chosen.

Stray and random thoughts will make every attempt to interfere with your concentration and distract you from your meditation. Don't allow it. Each time you realize your mind has wandered to other thoughts, acknowledge them, allow them to pass through your mind, then return to the subject of your focus. At first, it will be difficult to allow thoughts to pass through your mind without dwelling on them or chastising yourself for having them when you should be meditating. One of the great qualities of mediation is that it is non-judgmental. This means, simply, that whatever is happening is exactly what is happening, and it is neither good nor bad but should be accepted because it simply *is*.

The key to meditation, then, is the journey, not the destination.

As you practice repeating your mantra or concentrating visually on your object, usually you will find the stress and tension begin to lose their grip on your mind and body, and a sense of serenity and relaxation will replace them. This sense of serenity is not completely unlike what I saw in the Mahareshi's face on Merv's show over twenty five years ago!

You can meditate for as short or long a period of time as you wish. It is an amazingly flexible process. At first, you may wish to start small (five minutes, say), and if the process is successful for you, your meditation time may increase to as much as twenty or thirty minutes twice a day. It's entirely up to you.

Meditation has innumerable benefits in the classroom. When teachers are focused and their concentration is tuned to one thing at a time, their minds and bodies feel a greater sense of peacefulness while teaching, their projects get done with greater accuracy, and their students feel they are being listened to with greater intensity and sincerity.

Everybody wins!

With meditation, your mind is placed in the present and, therefore, any thoughts, concerns, or obligations from the past or future which are causing you stress or tension lose their significance in the moment as you are focused only on the "now." When you finish meditating, those responsibilities will still be there, of course, but you are more relaxed and comfortable and better equipped to deal with them in a more rational manner.

Many times the benefits of meditating spill over into our personal lives, as well. Recently, for example, I was at the dentist getting a filling replaced. When the drilling became especially high-pitched and the pressure on my teeth became uncomfortable, I simply went into a brief form of meditation. First, I took notice of my environment. I took stock of the physical condition of my body. My arms and legs were tight with tension, and my hands were gripping the armrest of the dentist chair. Next, while breathing through my nose, I got in touch with my breathing and began several deep, cleansing breaths. Then, while breathing in this manner, I found a spot on the ceiling (some irregularity in the stucco, as I recall) and began deep breathing in a gazing meditation. While the dental procedure was still no day at Disneyland, I was immediately able to relax physically and mentally and could handle the pressure and the drilling from a much calmer perspective. The whole process took less than five minutes, and the results were liberating.

Meditation has also served me well in my school environment. I had dropped my guard during our last spring break and did not come back as prepared as I usually like to be. I felt extremely disoriented our first morning back, had trouble remembering what ends I'd left loose, where I'd left off in certain lessons, and where certain books and worksheets were. I really had to search the hard drive in my mind to remember what we had done the week before spring break so I would be prepared when I got the inevitable requests for make-up work from pre-vacation absentees.

As first period loomed closer and closer, I felt myself getting more and more frantic about my upcoming obligations, and it began to have a physical effect on me. My breathing grew fast and shallow, my thinking blurred, and the structure of my preparation, which was panicked to begin with, broke down completely.

In short, I was stressing out!

It was time to meditate; time to, "think deeply, and quietly, to contemplate and to plan in one's mind." I stopped where I was, stopped what I was doing, acknowledged that first period was rapidly approaching (fifteen minutes and counting), and said to myself, "I need to do this, anyway."

I stood quietly for a moment, closed my eyes, got in touch with my breath impulse, not breathing until I felt the need and letting it come naturally based on my own personal breathing rhythm. Next I began to slow my breathing down, cleared my mind, and spent just a few minutes in deep thought and meditation.

When I opened my eyes, my breathing was more natural, even, and relaxed. My head was clear and I felt a sense of calm. It occurred to me that, in my panic and haste, I hadn't looked very carefully in my podium for that missing worksheet, so I walked slowly over to it, dug a little deeper this time, and ultimately retrieved the very thing I sought. After that, two other books I'd figured I'd left at home showed up on my desk. I remember more specifically where I'd left off with my classes and where I planned to take them. Most importantly, thought, I was physically much more relaxed and prepared for the day. My concentration was focused and I was thinking and seeing much more clearly. I was tuned in to my priorities, my purpose, and my environment.

Nothing had changed physically in the room.

The only thing that had changed was me.

It's no secret that preparation is the key to good teaching. It is, perhaps, more of a secret that every teacher has moments where he or she feels at a loss, unprepared, or in some way disheveled. This creates tension, which is the strongest anathema to a powerful and successful performance in the classroom.

You will benefit every day from a few minutes of contemplation, silence, and meditation. Stillness is a gift. And the best part is, you don't have to spend any time with The Beatles, talk to a quiet old man in a long, white robe, or twist yourself into the lotus position.

4

ATTITUDE

In my early days as a substitute teacher, I was filling in one day for a drama teacher in the same school district where I went to high school. The teacher was an old but venerated instructor who years ago had somehow appropriated the nickname "Doc." Doc had a conference to go to, and I was called to cover his classes for the day.

Much like an old film projector or file cabinet, Doc was a fixture in the district. I had often seen him before at official district functions or walking around the campus while I was subbing for other teachers at the same school. He was a big bear of a man, well over six feet tall and probably 250 pounds, with a shock of white hair and a medium length white beard. He always wore flannel shirts and big fisherman sweaters, at least those times I crossed his path, and that thick white hair was almost always covered by a navy blue fisherman's cap.

Doc slipped back into the classroom unobtrusively that day right before the last bell rang, returning to the theater for an after school rehearsal for the play he was directing.

After a brief description of my day, I mentioned I was an actor and a drama teacher myself, and Doc invited me to stay for the rehearsal. My steady diet of Top Ramen and rumors of his impending retirement was certainly enough motivation to get to know the place a little better, so I consented to sit in for awhile.

I don't remember the name of the play they rehearsed, but it was a musical. Clearly, they were in the early stages of the process, as there were no set pieces on the stage and all the actors were still glued to their scripts. As I found a seat in the house, they began running over dance steps and jotting blocking notes in their scripts. Right in the middle of a bit of choppy and half-hearted choreography, Doc suddenly stopped the action, leapt from his chair, and jumped directly on-stage.

"No, no, no, no," he said, shaking his head. "I don't *believe* you."

While I remembered frustrated directors shouting this phrase at many of the bewildered casts I had been a part of, I was not exactly sure where Doc was going with this.

"There is no passion," he yelled, "no commitment. You have to *sell* it. Watch."

Without warning, Doc launched into the same dance steps as if it were his first Broadway opening and his beloved grandmother was sitting in the front row of the theater. He had bright, twinkling eyes, a large smile, and an energy that would light half the city of Cincinnati.

What permeated Doc's impromptu performance, I remember, was the unmistakable sense that he was happy, that he was enjoying himself. He stopped the dance step cold on the last beat with a stomp downstage as smooth as a veteran hoofer, his hands extended for a beat—one slightly in front of his body, one slightly behind—to signal the end of the step.

I felt like bursting into applause. Some of the student actors standing around the panting professor did, but it was clear that they were used to Doc's displays.

What Doc was teaching all of us, I realized, was the importance of attitude, of "selling" your performance to the audience, using your technique to convince them they should be watching you because you're good at what you do and, more importantly, because you're enjoying the performance yourself.

"If you're not enjoying the performance," Doc chided his young charges, "then why the hell should they?"

It is no different in the classroom.

If, through your sense of attitude, you can sell your students on the message you are giving and its benefits, they will be more likely to want to listen and take something away with them. If you are enthusiastic about what you're saying and doing, that enthusiasm will be contagious and your students will catch the "bug."

This attitude of enjoyment and enthusiasm must be sincere and genuine. Forget the stereotypical fake smile and broad, hand-shaking, back-slapping attitude of the used car salesman, your students will spot that in a New York Minute. Instead, discover what it is that you like about your lesson, your message, sometimes even your career, and pass that along in the classroom through the vehicle of your attitude.

The right mood can make a class period reverberate with passion, energy, and vitality, while a poor one can cause it simply to crash and burn. Take, for instance, my usual experience with mythology. I hate mythology. I hated it when I studied it as a tenth grader, wading through Edith Hamilton's endless tome creatively titled *Mythology,* and I hate it every year that I teach it. I understand that we need to recognize the myriad of mythological references that we hear every day in our day-to-day lives—everything from Ajax Cleanser to Midas Mufflers; but otherwise, I never understood the appeal or the need. Frankly, there are too many names—many of which are virtually unpronounceable, the stories are too fantastic and unrealistic for my tastes, and it all happened so damn long ago. Who really cares if Prometheus was tied to a rock and a bird ate his liver? Or was that Perseus? Or was that the flying horse? Was that his Roman, Greek, or Norse name?

As teachers, we know how important it is to present the material with a sense of awe and wonder, regardless of our personal feelings. But it is difficult mustering even an ounce of zeal when it's a subject you so vehemently despise. As hard as I try to infuse my mythology unit with my fun and exciting attitude, it rarely—if ever—works as well as I would like. All teachers have certain sections of their subject they feel they do not teach very well, and mine is mythology. Every year I can sense my students' dissatisfaction for the way I present the material.

My only consolation is that I know there are pieces of literature that I love and teach with a strong and powerful sense of eagerness and spirit.

At my school, the English teachers are responsible for teaching three major literature units each semester. Recently, I polled my three freshman classes on their favorite literature of the semester. This semester we had read *Romeo and Juliet*, the mythology stories, and *Lord of the Flies*. The results shouldn't have surprised me, but they did. The students' favorite literature that semester was, resoundingly, *Romeo and Juliet*—the piece I love the most and feel I teach the best.

Their least favorite?

Exactly. Zeus and his buddies on the Mount.

While I do not blame the results of that vote solely on the basis of any bad teaching I've done, there is clearly a link between student interest and teacher attitude. I have to find something to like about teaching 5,000-year-old stories of Gods and Goddesses and pass that wonder on to the young faces wondering why their muffler shop is named after a greedy king.

Try this: Become your own stage director and watch your own performance. For one whole period, or even day, mentally stand over your own shoulder and observe the kind of attitude you present to your class. Don't be afraid to audio or videotape your class. Are you merely presenting the material in the same manner you have for decades or are you sincerely trying to "sell" them on a concept, piece of literature, or assignment? Is it an attitude of awe and wonder at the joy of learning, living, and experiencing knowledge? Is there a sense of passion and commitment. Have you generated suspense and mystery?

Or, are you doing what so many of the teachers we all had used to do: namely, do you slump through the door every morning and slog up to the lectern, running through the roll in a monotone voice usually reserved for train conductors calling off stops, then toss out the day's material with a sense of indifference and lassitude, reeking with the vibration that the only reason you bothered to show up is for the pitifully small paycheck?

You remember those teachers, don't you? Did you like them? Ask yourself how much you really learned from them. Ask yourself if you want to be that kind of teacher.

If you are not making every attempt to bring the material to life through your physical and emotional attitude, the students are not seeing your best stage work. Remember, this particular audience has never seen the show, and they deserve the most spirited, lively performance you are capable of giving.

Doc was right. Attitude counts.

5

STAGE FRIGHT

Every actor experiences stage fright. Performers who say they don't are either lying or are not approaching their performances with the right kind of energy. A certain amount of fear or anxiety is healthy for any performer. It is when the actor cannot function, when this anxiety paralyzes the performer to the point where the performance is in some way interfered with, that something must be done to eliminate the anxiety or fear.

Adrenaline, one of the best organic forms of energy we produce, should be coursing through an actor's veins before he or she steps out into the lights. This is normal. Every good athlete—from sprinter to race car driver—knows this feeling. So do the best actors and actresses. The key, as those professionals know, is what to do with this anxiety; how to channel it and focus it in the right direction. As performers—or teachers in a classroom setting—we can take anxiety about an upcoming performance and use it to rocket us directly through our fear and into an optimum state of power and confidence. If we learn to use our anxiousness correctly, we will walk into the classroom as finely tuned race cars, not the loud, smoky junkers our unbridled subconscious would have us feel like.

I have had absolutely numbing bouts of stage fright in my own experience as an actor. One summer, for example, I was performing with a group of people in a musical revue for the local theater awards show. We had an afternoon rehearsal for the show that evening. The run-through had been going very smoothly. This was only the second musical show in which I'd been cast, however, and I was not completely confident with my abilities in the song and dance department. Therefore, I still hadn't entirely squelched an underlying performance anxiety.

There were only a few hours before curtain. The rest of the cast had been very encouraging and supportive of my progress. I was having fun, but I was still very nervous, though, because we had just finished a dance step I was still working on and my big singing solo was coming up. After planting my feet after the dance step, I burst into singing my one solo line, only to look over and see Jamie, another singer, singing her line. Immediately, I realized I had come in woefully early. Jamie looked over at me, in mid-phrase, as if to say, "Why on earth are you singing during my solo?"

My confidence shut off like an old backyard hose. I apologized to Jamie later, and spent the few hours before showtime pacing, worrying, panicking, and fighting off waves of nausea. Doubts played through my head like songs on an oldies station: What if I did it again? What if my lack of skills ruined the show? What if they found me out for the fraud that I am, put me out on the street, and had the State Department in Washington exile me from the United State of America?

What then?

For moral support, I called my best friend from the pay phone in the lobby. She wisely reminded me that it was probably just nerves and that, even if I did do it again during the show, messing up my one singing line certainly wasn't going to ruin the entire production (in short, she put my performance ego back in check). As it turned out, I didn't miss my cue during performance, but those few hours before the show seemed an eternity.

I let my stage fright go unchecked during rehearsal, and it hamstringed me. During the performance, however, I allowed myself to relax and concentrate, and I focused my energy on my performance (instead of on my insecurities and what I *couldn't* do right) and the show ran smoothly and everyone, including me, had a good time.

The same approach will work for you in the classroom.

It is not uncommon for teachers to experience elements of stage fright. Many teachers talk of having dreams directly before school starts each year where they can't find their rooms, can't locate materials, or can't control unruly students. Then, of course, there is the perennial favorite—arriving at school clad only in a pair of boxer shorts or panties with the day of week stitched on the side. For those prone to nightmares, I suppose, it might even be the wrong day of the week stitched on the side.

For the first several years of my teaching career, I would find myself getting restless and anxious toward the end of our major vacation times: summer break, winter break, spring break. The negative tape loop in my brain—the one responsible for all the self-deprecating comments I hear in my head and heart—kept asking, "What if you've forgotten how to teach?" and "What if you face them on that first day and you have nothing to say?"

What should teachers do if they feel this unconfident, anxious, or panicked at the thought of approaching the classroom? They should go back to the relaxation exercises outlined in the beginning chapters of this book. Breathe. Meditate. Prepare. Teachers with "stage fright" should then focus the anxiety into positive energy and aim it toward the opening remarks of the week, the current lesson, or the unit at hand.

Each time we went back to school after a long break, I worked hard to tell myself that I would be fine, that I would know what to say to the class, and that I wouldn't forget what or how to teach. Fortunately, I have faith in my training—both in acting and teaching—and it has always came through for me. These days I don't hear that tape as much, but when I do, I take that tension, that *trapped energy* (which is what all tension is), and I focus it on preparing myself as thoroughly as possible so that I am completely confident and ready to teach.

I find the more thoroughly prepared I feel, the less anxiety creeps into my consciousness and, therefore, into my teaching, no matter when in the year that fear manifests itself.

The stage fright teachers feel as they step into the classroom is common, even normal, and just as real an actor's. Basically, we share the same experience as actors and actresses—that is, stepping out in front of an audience and wondering, day after day, if we're going to give a stellar performance or fall flat on our faces.

Chances are, we'll do a little of both.

BODY

6

PHYSICAL WARM-UP

When I was a young, earnest drama student at San Diego State University, I absorbed mountains of information regarding relaxation, breathing, and both physical and vocal expression. I learned a rigorous series of warm-ups which helped prepare me for both rehearsals and performances. One summer I was cast in a play in a local community theater. Being a dedicated student, I was determined to apply—too liberally, it turned out—all of the techniques I'd learned during my drama training.

The play was produced in the auditorium of a local junior high school. Before each night's performance, I would find a spot outside the auditorium, in the middle of the lunch area, near the metal tables where the students ate each day. After a moment or two of meditation, I launched into a regimen of physical warm-ups that would shame a Marine Corps boot camp. I did an exhaustive series of stretches, neck rolls, bends, arm circles, and leg lifts. I also executed face, eye, and mouth exercises that, to the untrained observer, probably made it seem as if I were having some kind of seizure. I implored my body to make me a loose, relaxed, and fluid performer.

I did this, purist that I was, in the name of Art.

Conversely, Shauna, the young woman who played my girlfriend in the play, walked on stage each night with what appeared to be zero preparation. Other than laughing and talking with fellow cast members in the dressing room or enjoying a quick cigarette out by the metal tables as she watched me twist and contort, she did virtually no warm-up whatsoever. Later, after discussing our contradictory styles, I discovered that she was jealous of my hands-on approach, while I confessed that I coveted her spontaneity. Interestingly, the truth of which method *was* most effective lies somewhere in between.

The same is true for teaching.

Some teachers come in five minutes before the final bell and wing their way through an entire impromptu lesson. While this can be exciting and spontaneous, using this method haphazardly can cause some teachers, who find they've run out of both time and ideas, to realize that they've backed themselves into a corner. Other teachers, however, will worry and fret months in advance of a particular unit or even, sometimes, an individual lesson. These instructors will expend so much quality energy in preparation that, by showtime, the lesson suffers from *too much* preparation and becomes stilted at best, or sometimes even dead-on-arrival.

Much like I should have done during my energetic explosions out by the lunch tables of that junior high school, teachers must determine what part of their bodies *need* to be relaxed, and what parts *exactly* need warming-up. Instead of putting every muscle in the body through the wringer of a physical warm-up whether it needs one or not, teachers should listen to their bodies and hear where they are tense or stressed. If the neck is stiff, do neck rolls. If the legs are tired or sore, work those muscles. This is a much more effective use of limited warm-up time than trying to work through every single muscle.

Teachers do not need to do a daily battery of calisthenics before they can be effective in the classroom. No one expects you to be the educational Richard Simmons. An effective physical warm-up, however, can lead to enhanced relaxation and relaxation is the key to optimum performances—whether you're performing for the season ticket holders of a community theater or during a final exam for thirty-five algebra II students.

The benefit to a good physical warm-up is two-fold. First, your body will have more mobility, less tension, and greater freedom of expression. That alone might make for a better day! Secondly, you will have more energy, as tension is merely energy that has trapped itself somewhere in the body. Warming up releases that energy so it can be used and channeled toward your performance in the classroom. This is a great advantage for teachers because if they have more energy, then the entire room becomes more electric and vitalized, creating a more energetic environment in which students can learn.

Take a few moments before school begins each day and sense where the stress has settled in your body. What areas of your body store up all the tension and anxiety that the day produces? For me, it tends to be in my shoulders and legs. For my wife, the base of her neck is like a stress magnet—it all concentrates where the head meets the spine and back and radiates across both shoulders. Listen to your body and discover where you keep all your anxiety locked up. Then release it.

Isolate the tension in your body, practice the breath impulse exercise from Chapter two, and then massage, roll, stretch, or knead those areas. Believe it or not, sometimes it helps to tighten certain muscle groups first, then as you release them, you can envision the tension flowing out of the bottom of your feet (or the ends of your fingertips) like water rushing down a stream or warm butter dripping down the side of a hot biscuit. Use whatever image works for you in order to visualize the stress actually *leaving* your body.

Start first by noticing where these problems exist. Listen to your body. Work only what *needs* to be worked. But, of course, check with your physician before undertaking any new exercise routine.

Head and Neck

Start by standing straight and tall. Drop your chin down to where it is almost touching your chest. Slowly roll your neck to the right, feeling for the pull and tug of the muscle. Work the muscle back and forth by rolling the neck all the way to the right and then all the way to the left. When you feel you've loosened those muscles sufficiently, drop your chin again. Tilt your head back, extending your chin upward. Feel your front neck muscles stretch. Then, tilt your head forward again, until your chin is almost touching your chest. Feel your back neck muscles stretch. Return your head to its usual upright position. Of course, these moves should all be done slowly at first, to allow you to adjust your comfort level.

Face

For improved facial mobility and expression, try this: Using the words "zero" and "rosy," over-exaggerate the pronunciation of each of these words, thereby using all of the muscles in your face to pronounce these words. Saying these words as "big" as you possibly can—amplifying the eyes, eyebrows, forehead, nose, mouth, cheeks, and chin—is a good way to stretch all of the muscles in the face. At some point during the exercise, stick your tongue out, feel it stretch, and then gently place it back in your mouth. Do this once or several times, depending on the stress level of the tongue. This not only stretches out the muscles in the face, but helps improve diction and enunciation as well.

Shoulders, Arms, and Hands

Nothing helps relax the shoulders like an old-fashioned shoulder roll. Standing straight and tall, place your arms at your sides, and begin to roll the shoulders forward in synch with each other. When they feel more loose, switch directions and roll them backward. Next, lift your arms above your head as if you were attempting to touch the ceiling and raise up on your tip toes. Stretch all of the muscles in your body toward the ceiling. After stretching, come back down on your feet and keep your posture straight. Next, keeping your feet shoulder width apart and your knees bent, lean to the right, lift your left arm over your head, and stretch out your left arm. In your arm and down your side, you will feel the "burn" that the workout people always talk about. That means it's working. When you lean to the other direction, make sure you shift your weight and anchor your leg in that direction. Then do the same with the right arm. Each time you return to an upright position make sure you keep your posture straight.

Small of Back

To stretch the lower back muscles, drop at the waist and stretch your arms to the floor. Next, with your hands on your hips bend back and feel the lower back muscles stretch. Under no circumstances should you overstrain these muscles. Just stretch until you feel the slight tug and pull that loosens and stretches them. Next, stretch your arms forward, wiggling your fingers wildly as if they were trying to separate themselves from your hands. Next, hold each wrist with the opposite hand and rotate on its joint, first one way and then the other, to loosen it up. Finally, roll the fingers of each hand. Beginning with your pinkies, raise and lower each finger and continue to roll them in a wave-like, circular motion—pinkie to index finger to pinkie to index finger. And so on and so on.

Legs and Feet

Feet. Start by rotating your foot on your ankle, first one way and then the other. Then, do the other foot. Next, tense the toes and release them. Tense and release. Tense and release. Do this until you feel the tension in your foot flow out of your toes or your heels.

Legs. Standing with your legs shoulder width apart, lift your right leg backwards and, while keeping your balance, hold it behind you with your right hand. While concentrating on your balance, lean forward until you feel the muscles in your upper thigh begin to stretch. Stop before it actually becomes painful. Next, do exactly the same thing with your left leg. If performed correctly, you will actually feel the stretch in both the upper thigh of the leg you're holding and the calf muscle of the stationary leg.

If you have the time, room, and inclination, you can also try the following leg stretch: sit on the ground. Next, spread your legs until they are shoulder width apart. Then, while keeping your back straight, extend your arms and flatten your hand, and try to touch your toes with your fingertips. First, lean toward the right foot and then lean toward the left foot. If performed correctly, you will feel the burn in the calf and bottom thigh muscles of the leg you are leaning toward. Perform until you feel the tension release and flow out of your legs through your feet.

Remember to begin all of these exercises slowly and work only to your own personal comfort level. Remember, too, that an effective physical warm-up can lead to a better mood, a better body, and a better teacher.

7

ENERGY

For educational purposes, energy can be defined as a sense of vitality, enthusiasm, and animation in the classroom. It is a liveliness and vigor in the performance of the teacher who keeps both the teacher and the students interested and engaged in the lesson. But it's hard to capture in words that feeling that emanates through a classroom that is run by a teacher with energy.

Energy is fuel. Energy is power.

Just like a car needs gas to run properly, people need energy to function throughout their daily activities—whether while on the job or after the whistle blows. People who stand up in front of other people for a living, however, need even *more* energy. The term "energy" refers not only to the amount of power and fuel to which you have access, but also to how you use it. Like money, energy can be spent wisely or foolishly. Like gas in a car, people can waste energy or conserve it.

A teacher can cultivate a sense of energy in the classroom in several ways.

An energetic teacher, for example, is:

Mobile

The energetic teacher is always on the go and frequently moves around the room. He or she keeps active and rarely sits. A mobile teacher is constantly aware of the surroundings, and is physically on the look out not only for trouble, but for moments for which a student should be praised, rewarded, or motivated to do more or to do better. To accomplish this, energetic teachers keep moving.

Able to Laugh

As you will see in the chapter on humor, the ability to laugh in the classroom is a gift. Energetic teachers find the delight in what they are doing and celebrate it. If your day among the students is sheer drudgery, quit and go sell shoes for your weekly paycheck. If you want to be an energetic teacher, however, find those moments that make you smile and be grateful for them. Then find those moments that make you laugh out loud and share that laughter with your students.

Furthermore, energetic teachers are not afraid to laugh at their own mistakes, gaffes, and foibles. Many times I have misspoke in class (sometimes implying, completely by accident, something off-color) and the class has burst into laughter. Instead of huffing and puffing and calling things back to order, I let myself appreciate the humor they are experiencing and join in with a good hearty laugh of my own; and sometimes that laugh is aimed directly at my own ego.

Be the kind of teacher who physically experiences the joy of being in the classroom.

Accessible

In the early-to-mid 1980's there was a movie called *Teachers* that depicted life in the "average" modern American high school. One of the teachers at the school was nicknamed "Ditto," for his propensity to use a worksheet curriculum. His students worked from bell to bell at their seats on pre-set worksheets while "Ditto" sat at his desk at the back of the room and read the newspaper. This daily routine was orchestrated to such a degree that Ditto had a massive coronary one day and died at his desk and no one noticed! The energetic teacher stays involved in what's happening in the classroom and is available for the students—for their questions, comments, critiques, and sometimes even their crises.

Energetic teachers do not wait for students to seek help, but rather they seek out students who need help, especially those who are too shy, confused, or immersed in the self-fulfilling prophecy of failure to bother to raise their hands to ask for the help they are already convinced will never come. Energetic teachers are not clock watchers (in fact, they are often engaged in the lesson to the degree that they are surprised when the bell rings), and they make themselves available to students during times outside the "typical" 50-minute period.

Open to Discussion and a Variety of Perspectives

There's nothing like a good old-fashioned debate to get some energy generated in the classroom. Energetic teachers welcome dialogue from the students, even if they disagree with each other. A teacher I work with was horrified to learn that if my interpretative questions go unanswered, I relish the "dead air" and let the silence hang for as long as it takes! The vacuum creates a healthy tension, and it is usually filled eventually with someone who needed the time to think of the excellent comment he or she finally makes. Don't fear the "dead air" in class discussion. Embrace it.

An energetic teacher also has the personal confidence to listen to points of view that do not merely parrot his or her own, instead welcoming dissent with the knowledge that the bandying about of divergent ideas will engage student interest and lead to a lesson brimming with vitality.

An energetic teacher also:

- interacts with students in a pleasant and positive way

- is earnest and sincere

- rests, eats right, and takes personal time to enjoy life outside the classroom

- frequently refers to students by name

- smiles a lot and asks about student's hobbies, families, and extra-curricular activities

Following these few guidelines will help any teachers generate energy in his or her lesson that will enliven the class. Students will become more engrossed in the activities and concepts of the day and will take more away from the classroom.

Energy can make your classroom lively, inspiring, and brilliant. Conversely, lack of energy can make it dismal, boring, and forgettable. There is a distinction, however, between teaching with energy that motivates, encourages, and gives students a sense of awe and wonder about the subject, and grabbing a hat and cane and merely "entertaining" students.

I learned about energy from a very unlikely source: the television evangelist.

Everyone who owns a television has seen an evangelist. I'm referring to the men—and more recently women—with the big hair, power suits, and earnest tones of voice who use the airway to spread The Word of God. Much like teaching, preaching has always reminded me of theater. It is a very performance-oriented experience, complete with performer, stage, and audience (not to mention lights, sound, costumes, and props.) These ministers shout, scream, beg, cajole, and run across the altar like sprinters, and often cry real tears in an effort to communicate their message to the audience.

Their goal is not only to get the audience to listen to, understand, be touched by, and agree with their message, but to literally *believe* in their message as well. We remember and are touched by the evangelist's message because his or her energy is so high, the intention so sincere, that we, as audience members, feel they are giving us the most important message anyone has every heard. These messengers behave with an enthusiasm and vitality that tells us we'd better listen. They access this energy during their performances and use it to grab our attention, keep us rapt, and shake us by our collars.

It is the energy of these messengers that fuels the lesson at hand. Can classroom teachers—who should be touting Shakespeare, polynomials, photosynthesis, and The Magna Carta as if they were as important as the Sermon on the Mount—settle for anything less?

8

BLOCKING

In acting, the term "blocking" refers to the movement of the actors across the playing area. A large part of the rehearsal process is spent with the director dictating exactly where an actor should be, on what line he should cross left, turn, say the next line, sit, rise, move downstage, gesture, and finally, exit stage right.

If the director is skilled, each movement is orchestrated to advance the director's "vision" of the play, to create a certain mood, or simply to construct an aesthetically pleasing composition on the stage, while always ensuring that each of the actors can be seen at all times.

Teachers rarely, if ever, consider blocking an important part of their daily routine. Because there are a number of significant and crucial issues for teachers to concern themselves with each and every day—legitimately, of course—the idea of planning when and where to move while teaching may seem a less important priority.

But it's not.

The effective use of movement in the classroom can make the difference between a mediocre lesson and one your students will remember. Like effective stage blocking, impressive, powerful movement in the classroom will go almost unnoticed—on the conscious level, anyway—the more expertly it is employed. Good blocking affects an audience subliminally and yet adds to their understanding, enjoyment, and appreciation of the whole production. Inspired blocking even has the power to touch a crowd's collective emotions. Effective movement can also echo, comment on, or underscore the point a performer is trying to make.

This is a powerful energy for a teacher to harness!

Imagine you are watching a stage play, for example, starring an excellent actor or actress. Imagine, now, watching that actor or actress spend the entire first act sitting on the sofa centerstage and the entire second act sitting stage right at the dining room table. Imagine there is little or no movement; that the ups and downs of the storyline are indicated only through the performer's voice and gestures. What would happen to the audience? Most likely they would fall asleep—just like the students who have teachers who are glued to their desks or lecterns and never move around the classroom, instead remaining motionless in front of the class, paralyzed as statues.

Not enough teachers get "out there" to communicate their messages. Many get trapped behind a desk, a podium, or a pointer and never use the space the classroom affords them. It is almost as if they are afraid to move around the room or to "get too close" to their students.

It is, quite frankly, the difference between teaching and telling.

Educators who are shackled to their "set pieces" like the poor, boring actor in the scenario above, send their audience into a deep apathy and, consequently, no matter how talented the actor (or teacher), *or how important the message*, the audience leaves knowing nothing more about the world than when they stepped into the theater (or classroom).

Blocking in the classroom also keeps things visually interesting. If the teacher never leaves the podium, the stimulus to continue listening is lessened and the students will quickly lose interest and go back to something more visual. Sheila will begin polishing her nails, for example, or Michael will go back to perusing the body-piercing magazine he has stashed in his backpack.

Using blocking in tandem with a number of other performance techniques mentioned in this book can keep the stimulus to learn very high and make the classroom a spontaneous and interesting environment in which to learn.

If the teacher moves to different positions in the room on key points, for example, and establishes eye contact with different students on each of the key points, and uses vocal inflection to further emphasize the difference between those key points, there is simply a better chance that the student will retain the material.

Powerful blocking will not only liven up your lessons, but it can also be used to illustrate critical relationships. For example, use your position in the room to show dichotomies. Move to the right to show the first side of a point or one end of the spectrum, and then physically move all the way to the other side of the room to illustrate the other end of the spectrum. Today, as it happens, I was teaching my students how to fix run on sentences by adding a coordinating conjunction (and, but, or so, yet). I said to them, "If there is one sentence over here," (I moved very far to my left and spread my hands out) "and another sentence over here," (and I moved very far to my right and spread my hands out again) "merely sticking a comma in between them is not enough." (I took two steps directly forward in the middle of the room and brought my hands close together as if were holding a small bird.) "You need a conjunction like and, but, or, so, nor, or yet to make the sentence complete." I used the space in the classroom to emphasize the concept I was teaching and used specific blocking choices that, with luck, helped clarify that grammatical point for my audience.

Using the space in the classroom this way creates a "visual" that the students can internalize which allows them to retain the material you are trying to communicate.

Not too long ago, I was not happy myself with my use of movement in the classroom. For a long time I could not figure out what the trouble was. I finally realized it was the placement of my desks. I operated for years within a traditional framework: all of my desks were in long, straight rows and I taught from a small, horizontal space in the front of the room by the white board and, when monitoring classwork, edged my way down the long, skinny rows.

One September, just before the school year began, I decided to move my desks into a series of three sections of three desks each: one to the right, one the left, and one against the back wall. This new configuration opened up the entire middle of the room for me to roam, to rant and rave, to communicate my message. It not only gave me space to function in as a teacher, but literally created a stage on which to perform. This new space allowed me to pace, to open up my body language, and to use almost all of the floor in front of me to "get out there." As an added bonus, whenever I had to give individual help, I only had to edge past two or three desks to get to any particular student. This arrangement also allowed me to sit on my haunches next to individual desks, thereby assisting each student at his or her level, not hovering over him or her like some behemoth. My eye contact became more meaningful, as we were able to look at each other eye-to-eye, both occupying equal physical position, which created a wonderful "working together" kind of attitude. I have felt the positive change in my classroom since making this change simply because this new arrangement of desks has opened up endless variations on my classroom blocking.

There are two basic rules regarding blocking in the classroom and they are the same as the rules for blocking in acting: 1) don't move too much and 2) don't move without motivation. In other words, know when to move and why you're moving.

Recently, I earned my Master's Degree in Educational Administration. For some reason, each class in the program insisted on a group presentation. One of the Master's candidates, a full-time working teacher himself, must have heard that movement in the classroom would keep things interesting and help students retain information. The only problem was that he didn't know when he had too much of a good thing.

This presenter moved so much and so frenetically, it quickly became completely distracting to his subject matter—almost comical, in fact. He walked in front of the desk, to the side of it, behind the desk, out in the classroom, back to the white board, all with no apparent purpose, motivation, or thought. He resembled one of those big, silver balls inside a pinball machine as it caroms off the lights and bumpers.

You may have noticed how silly it looks when actors move on stage or screen with no apparent motivation or goal for their actions. The poor Master's Degree candidate mentioned above proves that this is exactly how it looks in the classroom as well.

Blocking is one of the most easily overlooked of the performance techniques in this book to effectively incorporate into your daily lesson.

Make your class an interactive experience.

Get out there and move around.

9

EYE CONTACT

I once learned a very important lesson from a skinny, red-bearded wizard named Merlin.

At fifteen, I was cast in my first play—an abridged, children's theater version of *Sleeping Beauty*. I played Prince Charming. The script was a stream-lined, 75-minute version of the fairy tale which, inexplicably, included King Arthur's wizard, Merlin. It was my solemn responsibility to travel many miles and overcome a number of obstacles—including the simple task of conquering the power of evil—and with the help of a good fairy, a handful of magic roses, and Merlin, I was to seek out the sleeping princess and—what else?—wake her with a kiss. In retrospect, it reminds me of my college years, but that's another story.

In each of my many scenes with this wizard, I would be acting my heart out, wearing my "Princely" emotions on my sleeve like a teenage Al Pacino. I recited my lines, executed my blocking, even manipulated the magic roses so they appeared on cue to the "startled" audience.

Invariably, the time came during each rehearsal when Merlin, dressed in his outlandish, horsefly green, "genie-style" wizard outfit, would—without breaking character—take the first two fingers of his right hand, tap me on the shoulder in the middle of my line and, making a "V" with his two fingers, point my gaze directly into his eyes. He was never critical or impatient. He taught me a subtle, but extremely valuable lesson about communicating with other actors onstage:

Eye contact is everything.

I could have been out-Laurencing Olivier, and it wouldn't have made any difference. I was not communicating my message to my partner, the person to whom the message mattered the most.

In the classroom, the people who most need to hear the message are your students. In each class, we are always aware of the student or two who would benefit most from the information we are trying so industriously to pass along. Our job, then, is to find that student and look at him. *Really look at him*. Make eye contact and hold it for a moment until that student knows you've addressed something directly to him. Make it a conscious decision to connect with that student right then and there. Establish eye contact, and don't be the first one to look away. Yes, it's scary. Genuine communication is one of the most powerful things we do as human beings. That's why, as audiences, we are so riveted when actors do it onstage. Nothing was scarier, or more powerful, than looking directly into that wizard's eyes and telling him my story.

Now it's your turn.

A classroom can be a big place. So often teachers view each class as a unit, a single entity, a creature unto itself. They teach to the group mentality, but not to the individuals who contribute in their own way to the chemistry of that particular group. Start tomorrow. Make the classroom a little more intimate. Communicate a little more effectively by surveying the sea of faces, picking out a pair of eyes, and speaking directly to them. Then pick out another individual and give some of the message to her. Maybe she hasn't said much all year and you barely know her. Use this an opportunity to connect with each other over a lecture on photosynthesis, an explanation of The Versailles Treaty, or the magic of multiplying digits as if they were magic roses. Look at your students. Neither of you will ever forget the moment. Eye contact is that powerful.

When I was fifteen years old, a kindly, old wizard made me a better actor. It didn't occur to me until years later that he also made me a better teacher. There's an old saying that eyes are the windows to the soul.

If that's true, there are at least 70 windows in every classroom, every period that—I promise you—offer some dazzling views.

10

ACTIONS

In theater, action is everything. Inaction is deadly. Actors must be doing something for the audience to be interested. Choice is the key. The actor must choose the action that is appropriate to the character and the situation. From these actions, personality, emotion, and mood establish themselves and can be communicated to the audience. As Robert Benedetti says in *The Actor at Work,* "Do the action and the feeling will follow." Whether an actor is drinking coffee, shooting a gun, or hugging a child, each moment must be filled with action that allows the storyline to progress. Action advances the plot of a play as it unfolds on stage the same way it will move forward the content of a teacher's lesson plan.

Actions are most often expressed using verb forms. For example, I am going to *eat* an apple. I am going to *write* on the board. I am going to *stop* the film and *discuss* the social influence of Martin Luther King, Jr.'s' "I Have a Dream" speech.

Action is:

- What you do

- How you do it

- When you do it

Actions performed by teachers in the classroom should never be random or acts of chance. They should be specific, planned, determined, confident, detailed, and purposeful. They must also be appropriate to the subject matter, grade level, and lesson plan. Teachers who act on strongly specific, purposeful choices cannot help but enthrall their audiences.

There are strong actions and weak actions. Strong actions are specific and have a specific purpose in mind—a goal or objective the teacher wishes to achieve. Weak actions are vague, generalized, or random. There is no evident purpose for doing them.

Here are some examples:

Weak Actions	Purpose	Strong Action
Wandering aimlessly around the room during a lecture.	Check understanding of material	Walking through the classroom to monitor work and determine which student(s) need help
Writing on the board during a lecture, but facing the board while you speak.	Communicating the material to *all* learners	Establishing eye contact with individual students during a lecture.
Only erasing a small portion of the already messy board to write a new concept on it.	Teaching material Clearly and effectively	Erasing the entire board before writing down a new idea.

In the first example of the strong actions, the objective is clear: to monitor work and determine student needs. Conversely, in the example of the weak action, it is obvious that while wandering around the room during a lecture is, in fact, an action, there is no purpose for it and it does not meet a specific objective. The other strong actions are powerful choices for actions because they have a definite purpose, they foster clear communication, and they allow the teacher to meaningfully connect with students. The weak actions, on the other hand, have no clear objective, so they obviously impede (or at the very least cloud) clear communication, and keep students guessing. Ask yourself which choices are going to help students learn. Despite the fact that there are teachers whose styles would infinitely improve if they took any action at all, the weak action should be immediately recognizable as the inferior choice.

Let me give you an example of a strong action that is appropriate to a particular lesson plan. Each year I teach my freshmen *Lord of the Flies,* by William Golding. In this social commentary masquerading as an adventure story, the plane-wrecked boys call assemblies by blowing into a conch shell. The loud, resonant bellowing of the shell calls the boys from various ends of the island on which they are stranded, so they can meet and discuss plans for rescue.

After I'm certain my students are clear on how the boys use the shell in the book, I place a conch shell on the desk in my office (which is adjacent to my classroom). When the bell rings, I take roll. Then as if to call the assembly to order, I walk into my office, pick up the conch shell, reenter the classroom, and blow until my face turns beet red.

Not only does this deliberate action cause students to snap to attention (frankly, it even scares a few who weren't quite paying attention yet), but it is also a highly dramatic action that engages my "audience." They will also then know that this will not be like all the other classes we've had together. Next I split the class into two groups, give each group a conch shell, and tell them that no one can speak unless he or she has the conch shell (exactly the rule the boys were required to follow on the island.). Immediately, they identify with the situation in the book because the lesson began with a strong action. Using the conch shell in the beginning of the period to increase interest, I segued from a strong, specific action into the lesson for the day and underscored themes of authority, order, and civilization found in the novel.

Strong actions are also important in other subject areas as well, whether it is a physical education teacher demonstrating the proper technique for spiking a volleyball, a math teacher writing steps in a problem clearly and legibly on the board, or a science teacher showing students the steps in an experiment.

The only exception to the idea of using strong actions is this: Sometimes the strongest action is no action at all. I am reminded of a particularly frenetic musical I once saw where in one scene a young woman came out on stage to sing a solo. Unlike the rest of the show, the song was slow, sensitive, and ultimately, poignant. To underscore this, the director chose to have her sing the entire song center stage, while standing absolutely still. In a show where the rest of the action looked like something out of a Three Stooges short, this unexpected lack of action was emotionally moving.

This trick can also work well in the classroom. If you have been teaching a fast-paced, energetic, and passionate lesson, and you know a significant and meaningful concept or point is coming up, just as you reach that moment, pick a spot in the room (preferably one that has good sightlines from every seat in the house) and stand completely motionless. The contrast of action to no action will electrify your audience.

In short, stillness can be an incredibly powerful action.

Action, ultimately, is the doing of something.

Do something important.

VOICE

11

VOCAL WARM-UP

The beginning of a new school year has a way of sneaking up even on the most alert teachers. Suddenly, there are a million things to be done in those precious few days before showtime. Before we know it, classrooms are organized, staff meetings have adjourned, and it is time to welcome the fresh new faces back for another year of learning.

How many of us, though, fail to adequately prepare ourselves physically for that first day? How many of us, at the end of that first grueling day, hear the final bell, watch the class empty like an hourglass, and then find our bodies tired, our muscles out of energy, and our voices ragged and hoarse, having gone three months since using—in a professional manner, anyway—our most precious instrument for communication?

While some form of vocal warm-up is probably a good idea every day, it is particularly necessary for teachers to prepare their voices after they have been away from the classroom "stage" for any length of time. The best way for teachers to be in optimum shape for their performance in the classroom is to do a physical and/or vocal warm-up any time they feel tension, stress, or lack of energy.

A vocal warm-up that prepares a teacher for a day in the classroom is a very simple process. Educators do not need to spend each morning running a series of "me-me-me-me-me's" or "red leather/yellow leathers" as if they were Luciano Pavarotti or Placido Domingo warming up to sing a lead at The Met. Leave that to The Three Tenors.

On the other hand, imagine you are a great concert violinist. Now imagine the care, reverence, respect, even love with which you treat your treasured violin. Perhaps it is even a Stradivarius. You tune it carefully and regularly, you clean it with a soft cloth, you keep it protected in its case each time you are finished playing, you replace the strings and tuning knobs, and you do everything in your power to insure the violin is well taken care of and prepared to work its magic each and every performance.

In teaching, you are the violin.

Your body and voice are the two instruments that give the performance, play the melody, create the music. Wouldn't it make sense, then, to take good care of these instruments, tune them regularly, and keep them in the best possible shape every time you face your audience?

An average vocal warm-up consists of a few exercises designed to help you produce and project sound clearly and accurately. The warm-ups will focus on those parts of the body that produce sound: mouth, teeth, lips, tongue, throat, diaphragm, chest, and nose.

The following exercises have been modified for use in the classroom and can be as simple or complex as necessary. Do any exercise individually or use them as part of a vocal regimen. Do them quickly or take your time. The key, much like with the physical warm-up, is to identify which parts of your voice need a nudge toward peak performance.

The progression of warm-ups focuses on the following:

- The breath

- The vocal instrument (sound)

- The articulators (lips, teeth, and tongue)

- The middle sinus and chest resonators

Sigh

The first step is to get in touch with the breath. An easy way to do this during the beginning of a vocal warm-up is to sigh. Open your mouth, and just imagine that the breath drops in quickly, feel it sink all the way to your belly, and then thoroughly expel it through your open mouth. The whole process takes about a second and a half. You should sigh three or four times to get the breath rushing between your chest, your mouth, and through your lips and teeth. As you begin to feel comfortable enough eventually, it is a good idea to vocalize on a sound as you sigh. For example, vocalize on an "ahhhhhh," "haaaaaa," or "heeeeeee" sound.

Yawn

Open your mouth wide and send air out in a simulated yawn (It usually starts as a simulation, anyway, but you will often find yourself actually yawning before you know it!). Pretending to yawn is a great way to relax your breathing. Another benefit to yawning is that it opens up the passageway between the diaphragm, chest, throat, and mouth, creating a superhighway of sound. When you have practiced the vocal warm-up a number of times and are feeling less self-conscious, it helps to vocalize on a sound (usually an open-throated, "ahhhhhhh" sound). Yawning is a great way to access the breath and begin to feel in tune with your voice.

Hum

The best time to start this exercise is in the car on the way to work. Turn on the radio, find a song you like, and begin to hum to the song for several minutes. Make sure that you hum at different volumes and at different pitches. Next, focus the humming in your nasal cavity (it should vibrate or "tickle" in your nose), then in your mouth, and finally in your chest. Humming sends vibrations through the mouth, nose, throat, and chest that begin to wake up the sleepy body parts that make up your voice. Even by itself, humming is a quick way to make your voice performance-ready.

The Nasal Cavity (middle sinus resonators)

This exercise is performed by beginning with the humming exercise, vocalizing on an "mmmmmmm" sound and then focusing the hum up into the nasal cavity. While humming and vocalizing, raise your two index fingers to your nose and begin massaging the areas to the right and left of the bridge of the nose. This warms up the middle sinus resonators and allows the sound to resonate in your nasal cavity, which helps produce a richer, fuller sound. (Warning: It's wise to have a tissue handy. This technique warms up the nasal cavity so well, it usually tends to cause the nose to run).

The Chest (chest resonators)

While vocalizing on an "ahhhhh" sound, take your clenched fists and pound lightly on your chest cavity. Cover your entire chest with your fists—wherever you feel the sound vibrating. This pounding wakes up the whole chest and chest area and gives your voice greater resonance in the chest cavity. You may feel a bit like Tarzan, so it may be best to do this exercise alone, in order to save lengthy explanations to curious onlookers.

Blowing the Lips

Do this just like you've seen your two-year-old niece or nephew do on his or her holiday visits. Blow air out through your mouth, without parting your lips. You will create a sound very much like what is sometimes called a "raspberry" or "Bronx Cheer," which is precisely what you want. The benefit here is that blowing your lips wakes up the groggy or lazy articulators by creating vibrations on the lips, teeth, and mouth. When the articulators are warmed-up and ready for action, not only is the voice more clear, but the performer's diction is more precise. This technique works particularly well when used in tandem with the humming exercise.

The Tongue

The tongue, another one of the articulators, can be warmed up by rolling it in and out of the mouth. Begin by placing the tip of your tongue in a comfortable and relaxed position directly behind the bottom teeth. Next, push the tongue out so that the bulky middle part is pushed out of your mouth, past your parted lips. Make sure your jaw drops comfortably and that you are not forcing your tongue out stressfully, but rather allowing it to stretch like a cat who has just awakened from a deep sleep. Repeat this process at least 8-10 times in rapid succession, then place the tongue back in the mouth in a comfortable and relaxed position. This technique relaxes the tongue, gives it greater freedom of mobility, and allows it more dexterity in pronouncing words.

These exercises should warm-up the voice adequately and prepare you for a day in the classroom. If certain parts of your voice are experiencing extra stress or tension, spend a little more time on that area of your body or that part of the voice. The teacher, much like the stage performer, must learn to relax and exercise the voice in order to express a variety of messages, ideas, and emotions.

Teaching is about communicating ideas, and since much of the communicating teachers do is with their voices, it is critical that they exercise and protect this delicate instrument, as if it were their very own Stradivarius and they were on their way to Carnegie Hall.

12

PROJECTION

Projection is the ability to fill a performance space with full, clear sound. We've all experienced teachers, speakers, or presenters who have not perfected the skill of projection. As a result, we find ourselves moving closer, leaning in, and ultimately missing much of the information. Furthermore, poor projection weakens the speaker's credibility. The audience may consider him or her not as professional, less skilled or knowledgeable, sometimes even nervous, weak, or afraid. When we cannot hear someone who purports to be passing along critical information, we doubt his or her veracity.

Projection is a simple concept (I can either hear you or I cannot) and a relatively easy skill to learn and practice. Yet so many teachers speak only to the first row of students, ignoring the rest of the room, and forcing the rest of their listeners to struggle and fight for their fair share of the lesson. Students should have to work diligently in the classroom, yes, *but not at hearing what the teacher is saying*. Students have plenty of distracting and frustrating circumstances interrupting their learning processes; they shouldn't also have to contend with teachers they cannot hear.

Projection should not be confused with yelling or shouting. Projection is about power, not volume. It is about finding the strength and modulation in your voice that will carry it a great distance and still allow it to retain the power it possessed when the words left your mouth. This strength and power comes from placing the breath and sound all the way down in the diaphragm. After being carefully and strongly supported by the breath, the voice must then, through excellent diction, be clarified by the lips, teeth, and tongue. The voice should be made still more expressive through inflection, emotion, and passion.

A Simple Exercise in Projection

To fully understand the distinction between shouting and projection, try this: place the palm of your hand flat against the middle of your stomach. Take a breath and let the breath drop in all the way down until you feel it filling up your belly. Next, vocalize on the word, "Hey!" as if you are attempting to stop a young boy from stealing an apple from the market across the street. Let the voice rise up from your stomach like water through a faucet until it gushes out of your mouth. Let it build from the diaphragm, and then launch it out of your mouth like a rocket. The reverberation of your voice should rock you. It should feel different than when you are yelling or shouting (or talking normally, for that matter). Powerful projection should make you feel as if your voice has ricocheted off your skeleton and filled your whole body with sound. The inside of your head should hum with the intensity of your voice. The sound quality of that single syllable ("Hey!") should fill the air with depth and power.

This is projection.

The teacher's professional obligation is the transmission of ideas. The voice and the body are two of the most important vehicles through which this transmission occurs. Certainly books, worksheets, projects, films, and peer interaction are critical as well, but if they were the most important parts of teaching, the students could stay at home for twelve years, fax in their homework, and receive a diploma via e-mail. We expect them to rise early, eat their Wheaties, and arrive at school punctually because we value the connection they have with the mentors they encounter each day; mentors who are older, more experienced and, presumably, wiser.

A teacher's message must be heard. If what you say in the classroom, and how you say it, wasn't important to your students, then they wouldn't have to show up every morning.

And neither would you.

13

DICTION

"Speak the speech, I pray, as I pronounced it to you, trippingly on the tongue; but if you mouth it, as many of your players do, I had as lief the town-crier spoke my lines."

—*Hamlet, III, ii*

Proper diction is one of the most critical aspects of a teacher's performance technique. Increase the clarity of your voice and, by default, you increase the clarity of your message. It's a "can't miss/can't lose" approach. A message cannot be understood correctly if it is not received correctly. Diction (also known as enunciation or articulation) is the art of pronouncing words precisely, of speaking in a clear and distinct manner. In lay terms, diction involves hitting all of the sounds in a word and not swallowing any. Many speakers, actors, and teachers often are difficult to understand, early in their careers, because they have not developed the full potential of their diction.

Diction works in tandem with projection to ensure a teacher's message is being communicated. Actors spend much of their time making certain their voices are finely-tuned instruments so that, using the tools of diction and projection, they are better able to convey the depth, nuance, and meaning of words and the full the spectrum of emotions.

Why should teachers settle for less?

Imagine sitting in a class and trying to learn from a teacher whose words you could not understand, no matter how hard you tried. Taking notes would be a nightmare—guessing at words or meanings, scribbling fragments of ideas, hoping you had the right information, constantly leaning over to the person beside you and whispering, "What did he just say?"

This is no way to learn.

Beginners are used to speaking conversationally for one or two people standing or sitting very near. In this instance, it is not so critical to enunciate words as precisely because the listeners are so close they probably know the idiosyncrasies of the speaker's voice, so they don't have to listen as closely to decode the meaning; they can intuit it. How many of us, for example, wondering aloud if are friends have had any lunch or dinner yet, have innocently inquired, "Jeet?" Almost all of us have either said this or heard other ask it of us. We understood the monosyllabic utterance as the question, "Did you eat?" Consequently, no explanation is really necessary. The speaker's intent is clear. If any words are lost, an educated guess on the part of the listener is usually good enough to divine the speaker's meaning.

Actors, however, are not afforded the luxury of relying on audience guesswork; nor can teachers rely on such student guesswork in the classroom. Their message must be carefully sculpted and precisely presented—the first time—largely through the art of diction.

Missing Sounds

We can improve our diction by beginning to understand which sounds we are likely to be missing, leaving out, swallowing, or mispronouncing. Where I live in Southern California, for example, people have a habit of pronouncing the word g-e-t as, "git," as in "I'm going to go to the store and git a newspaper." Hitting the "e" in "get" (it should rhyme with "bet") is not something many people in this locale are accustomed to doing. My drama teachers drilled "git" out of my vocabulary early in my training. Something as simple as saying "get" instead of "git" can make your speech, and therefore your message, so much easier to understand.

Similarly, many sloppy speakers will clip the word, "to," and pronounce it "ta" or "da." To use our previous example, many people would say, "I'm going da go ta the store da git a newspaper." The minor adjustment of changing an "a" sound to an "o" sound and saying "to" instead of "ta" will go along way toward making your message easier for your listeners to receive and understand.

Furthermore, we all know how poor diction leads to turning "going to" into "gonna," and "want to" into "wanna." We then end up with "I'm gonna go da the store da git a newspaper." Or, taken to its logical extreme, we hear "I'm gunagoda da sto' n git a 'papah." The further we go, and the sloppier our speech, the less our sentences sound like they're being spoken in English, or any intelligible language for that matter.

There are other sounds that individual speakers either drop or ignore altogether. Discover the gremlins in your own speech patterns (audiotape a class period, if necessary) and banish them.

Hitting the Hard Consonants

Hitting hard consonants is another element of good diction that many speakers neglect. Hitting the "d," "t," "k," "p," sounds, especially at the ends of words, will improve your diction immensely.

Take the sentence, "How nice to meet you, Mrs. Harcourt." Aside from missing the "o" in "to," poor diction would lead us to drop the "t" sound in "meet" and lazy speakers would hope to get away with "meecha." We might also drop the "t" sound in "Harcourt." At its most base, then, this sentence might ultimately be spoken as "How niceta meecha, Mrs. Harcour'." Clear separation of sounds in our precise speech and clear pronunciation will guarantee proper diction. We should say, "How nice *to* mee*t* you, Mrs. Harcour*t*."

Hard consonants must be hit strongly and clearly, especially when they appear at the end of a word.

A Quick Exercise in Diction

If you arrive to the classroom and feel you are going to have an unusu-ally mush-mouthed day, there is an amazingly simple exercise that will significantly—and immediately—improve your diction.

Try this: Pick up something you can read aloud. Actors would use their scripts, but you can use a novel, textbook, or the daily newspaper. Even children's nursery rhymes would work. Start with "Mary Had a Little Lamb" if you must, but find something you can speak aloud. Use whatever's close at hand. First, stick your tongue out as far as it will go. Next, practice speaking the words on the practice page as clearly as you can, but continuing to speak while your tongue is extended as far as it will go ("Mahhy hab uh ittle amb, ittle amb…"). This exercise not only warms-up the voice and the articulators (lips, teeth, and tongue), but forces the sounds to come to the front of the mouth where they belong. This placement requires each sound to be clear and precise.

After speaking for a few moments in this fashion, pull your tongue back in your mouth and try the piece a second time, again attempting to speak as clearly as possible. I guarantee in the second reading, you will notice a palpable improvement in your diction.

This exercise is best done after a vocal warm-up (see chapter 11), but it's a great diction pick-me-up in the middle of the day when the mouth gets tired or lazy. Even your late afternoon students deserve your best enunciation because, remember, they haven't seen the show yet.

These few examples should illustrate how muddy our speech pat-terns can git (sorry, uh, I mean get), if we're not careful. In casual con-versation or street talk, of course, these rules are not as important. Teachers, however, cannot afford the kind of vocal laziness of cocktail party chatter or basketball court banter. Teachers are in front of an audience every day that needs to understand—clearly and dis-tinctly—what we are trying to say. While you shouldn't feel the need to speak like Kenneth Branaugh or Anthony Hopkins, speaking as clearly, precisely, and ultimately, as beautifully as they do never hurts.

14

INFLECTION

During my first year in college I had a very bright and creative drama teacher. One of the most valuable concepts he taught his students about performing concerned speaking our lines. He walked into the classroom one day and announced he was going to teach us to "use our words."

He explained that using our words referred to giving them nuance, meaning, color, and emotion, simply by adjusting the way in which they are spoken. Using our words referred not only to making certain our words reached our audience, but that how we felt about what we were saying reached them, too.

We were learning, as it turned out, the power of inflection.

Inflection consists of assigning value and meaning to individual words—deciding which are important and worth emphasizing and which are less important and should be skimmed over. Simply put, inflection is the learning to express the quality of a word through the manner in which you say it.

This ability to communicate the emotional tone of a sentence using only the voice can make the difference between a memorable lesson, lecture, discussion, or reading that inspires your students and one which simply puts them to sleep or drives them back to their Game-Boys or *Monster Truck Monthly* magazines. Establishing an emotional tone with your voice, and then reinforcing the message with appropriate physical movement, body language, and blocking will increase the force and effectiveness of each lesson and add currency to your stage presence in the classroom.

There are three aspects of inflection you should concern yourself with: emphasis image, and connotation.

<u>Emphasis</u>

I began to see the full importance of this concept in my English classes during a recent unit on mythology.

Mythology, as I tell my students, was primarily passed on using the oral tradition. The ancient Greeks and Romans did not have radio, television, film, DVD, or The Internet. They were forced to rely almost solely on the entertainment value of the stories they told. In this manner, they passed on certain universal truths about love, moral conduct, religion, and duty. These stories of strength, passion, and spirituality relied on fantastic and, often, terribly violent imagery to keep their listeners rapt with attention. As students of mythology already know, these stories frequently told of horribly violent battles, deaths, beheadings, dismemberments, and various and sundry tortures. For example, Prometheus was tied to a rock so a bird could eat his liver only to have the organ regenerate so the bird could dine on it again the very next day. Today's most violent movies and graphic television shows have a hard time competing with the images from even the tamest of the ancient myths.

The more graphic the image, the more precise the word choice, and the better the storyteller had to be at the art of inflection to increase the likelihood that the listener would come away having learned the lesson; therefore, storytellers relied almost exclusively on the strength and skill of their voices to communicate the message *and the attitude toward the message* by using the words in powerful and emotional ways.

One mythology text we use at our school is *Mythology and You* by Donna Rosenberg and Sorelle Baker. In "The Rule of Uranus," one of the origin of the universe tales, Uranus' son, Cronus, is about to kill his father and take control of the universe. In the version we use, there is the following line:

"Cronus mutilated his father and threw the severed parts into the sea."

An unskilled reader might give each of the words in that sentence equal value, completely suppressing all of the dynamics, power, and violence the author intended his audience to enjoy, as well as from which to learn. Conversely, the skilled reader would carefully choose the words that *matter* and emphasize each one accordingly (informally we call this "punching"—as in "I'm going to *punch* the word 'mutilated'."). While it may seem as if you must painstakingly diagram each sentence using spreadsheets, bar graphs, and pie charts, that just simply isn't so. Usually, it means having a copy of the text that you can write on. Simply underline, highlight, or otherwise mark the words you want to punch so that when you read, the most important words are clear at a glance, and you can give them the emphasis and weight they deserve as you speak them.

Good writing depends on strong verbs. Begin then, by marking the action words. Isolating the verbs that depict strong actions and punching those would be a good first step toward "using your words" effectively.

While everyone makes different performance choices (This is why actors have different performance styles and why acting is considered an art), there are certain absolutes. Emphasizing the verbs is one of those absolutes. In the sentence above, for example, the verb "mutilated" should be given some emphasis, as follows:

"Cronus **MUTILATED** his father and threw the severed parts into the sea."

This emphasis sets the action apart and gives it value. Cronus didn't "cut" his father, he didn't "slice" his father, he didn't "julienne" his father, he *mutilated* him. That word is chosen specifically because of the uncontrolled violence it suggests. It should also be emphasized because of its powerful connotation and strong sense of imagery it conjures up in the listener's mind. As you can see, the three parts of inflection frequently work together.

There are other words in this sentence to which we can add color, seasoning, personality, and verve. At a quick glance, the other words (my personal choices, that is) would be "threw," "severed," and "sea." The word "threw" would get a little punch simply because it is a verb. "Severed" is a strong, descriptive word and creates an image for the reader to visualize (more on that in a moment). Finally, as one of my director's always admonished her cast to "keep the ends of the sentences UP!," the word "sea" should be hit somehow strongly. Not only is "sea" also a descriptive, image-provoking word, but it gives the listener a setting. It answers the "Where are we?" question and, therefore, should be clearly communicated.

The sentence above might be read something like this:

"Cronus **MUTILATED** his father and *threw* the **severed** parts into the Sea."

The most important words ("mutilated") is in boldface and all caps, the other verb ("threw") is in italics because it is noted, but punched less strongly, the next image word ("severed") is bold-faced lower case because you hit it like mutilated, but not as strongly and, finally, the end of the sentence is kept up which is represented by the last word ("Sea") being capitalized.

I am not suggesting that teachers speak abnormally or twist the texture of their voice like some sideshow contortionist. Speak normally, but give your reading or lecture or discussion a rhythm, a music, that allows different words and phrases to carry different values, gravity, and timbres—all of which support the message being communicated.

This technique is useful not only for sentences that have violent or graphic images, but for any sentences that have strong imagery or vivid figurative language. Performers can create a sense of poetry, beauty, joy, or sadness by using the words in a sentence that convey those messages.

Author John Steinbeck's novel *The Grapes of Wrath,* for example, begins:

"To the red country and part of the gray country of Oklahoma, the last rains came gently, and they did not cut the scarred earth."

As an exercise, write this sentence on a piece of paper you can mark up. Next, identify and mark the words you wish to emphasize and use symbols you'll understand to mark certain rhythm or pace indicators (such as dashes, commas, backslash marks, ellipses, etc.) and then read the sentence aloud.

Choosing the right words to emphasize will add depth and development to each piece you read in the classroom or, for non-English teachers, will add layers of meaning that you have specifically chosen to communicate to your math, foreign language, or social science students.

Imagery

Imagery refers to the word pictures that the writer paints with his words. Images usually appeal to one of the five senses—seeing, hearing, tasting, touching, and smelling. Images allow us to visualize passages of text as we read or listen. I tell my students to identify the imagery in a piece so that they can "play the movie in your mind."

In the sample sentence, the phrase "severed parts" creates an image that appeals to the sense of sight. We can see in our mind's eye, perhaps, dangling limbs and chunks of meat (okay, I'll stop) falling from the heavens and crashing into the ocean. Therefore, another choice for emphasis in a selection you're reading or a discussion you're giving would be to punch the imagery. Many times the imagery is created by the use of comparisons. In other words, look for similes and metaphors in order to dig out the imagery.

Now go back to the emphasis exercise sentence from *The Grapes of Wrath*. Make an identifying mark on the image words—in this case, "red," "gray," "rains," "cut," and "scarred." The first two words are colors which are always visual images, while the word "rains" can actually be a sight, sound, and touch image. It is possible to see rain, hear it falling, and feel its wetness on your skin. And, finally, "cut" and "scarred" are touch images that suggest pain, and once again invoke a certain sense of violence that these poor people had to experience during the great Dustbowl period of the early thirties. In the case of this sentence, punching the image words will go a long way toward helping you communicate the sad story of the Joad family in a powerful and poignant manner.

Connotation

Connotation is another concept to consider when using your words. Words have qualities, associations, and may carry meanings which are expressed in the sound of word, even if they are not part of the literal dictionary definition (also known as "denotation"). The key for teachers, as performers, is to say the word in such a way that meaning, quality, or association is carried through the sound to the listener's ear. The word "heat," for example, can mean simply that the temperature is very high. It can also connote anger, passion, oppression, lust, or pressure. Performers can use their vocal inflection to convey any of the listed connotations or any other message they think is being communicated by a word. The performer should suggest in inflection (and body language) a sense of the "hotness" of the word, the intensity, the sweatiness, the enveloping thickness of air one feels during periods of great heat.

All of this can be communicated through the use of that one word. The key is how you say it.

Try this: Copy the following paragraph so that you can write on it. Using symbols that will make sense to you personally, mark the words in a manner that will indicate which words you intend to emphasize and how. Then speak the paragraph out loud, being certain to use the action words, the descriptive words and phrases that evoke strong images, and the words with powerful connotations:

Last night for dinner, I had a sizzling sirloin steak fresh from the grill, covered in simmered mushrooms, with a piping hot baked potato, drowning in butter, tart sour cream, and crispy chives. Also on the side, I had fat, green broccoli flourettes dripping with cheese sauce. I drank a tall, cold glass of whole milk (none of that watery, skim stuff for me!) and, for dessert, I polished off half of a French Crumb Apple Pie topped with melting vanilla ice cream.

Practice this paragraph several times, choosing to punch different words each time. The fun part is that each performer will personally choose which words to emphasize and which words to de-emphasize, depending on the message he or she intends to communicate. Sometimes it will be painfully obvious you have chosen the wrong word, just as it is clear when a pianist, guitarist, or singer hits a wrong note in the middle of a song. This can be valuable, too. You can discover new meaning from the words, from the sounds, even from the sentence itself—all of which alert you to the possibilities inherent in the individual words. Then, you can coax out these new meanings and give your lectures greater depth, insight, and nuance.

Make using your words a personal teaching choice, whether in a reading, individual instruction, or during a lecture. With practice, even impromptu anecdotes or explanations of concepts can be livened up by the correct inflection and word emphasis.

Use your words. Don't let them use you!

15

CHARACTER VOICES

o o o o o o o o o o o o o o o o o o o o o o o o o o o o o o o

Warning: Non-Literature teachers may wish to take a short coffee break…

Remember those old Warner Brothers cartoons? They contained some of the most clever and literate jokes on film and starred many of the most entertaining characters ever to appear in animated form: Daffy Duck, Porky Pig, Sylvester and Tweety, the Road Runner and Wile E. Coyote, Yosemite Sam and, of course, the ringleader of the bunch and my personal favorite, Bugs Bunny. I still remember how amazing it was to learn that all of those wildly different, yet singularly individualized voices came from one person—the legendary Mel Blanc.

I specifically remember being very entertained as a child by the Abominable Snowman who co-starred in one of the Bugs Bunny cartoons. He was a large, brutish character and was—as they say—not exactly the sharpest tool in the shed. This snowman decides, upon finding Bugs near his mountaintop home, to adopt him as a pet and vows to "love him, and pet him, and feed him." Years later, it dawned on me that this character was an affectionate homage to Lennie, the sensitive, but mentally challenged, giant in *Of Mice and Men*, a book published during roughly the same era as this "icy" cartoon character. It is this voice, I admit in writing, that I imitate for the part of Lennie when I read to my ninth grade students from Steinbeck's short novel.

Using character voices while reading literature aloud to your students not only makes your performance more interesting and riveting, but gives it depth and resonance as well by creating the very powerful illusion that there are many people up in front of the classroom, instead of the same individual teacher who is behind the lectern every day of the week. One of the most enjoyable aspects of my job is reading literature aloud to students and using different voices, postures, and attitudes for the various characters.

I am not naturally adept at character voices. They aren't always easy to develop or perform. I always admired many of my actor friends who had a wide repertoire of voices they could pull from, seemingly at a moment's notice. Frequently, they would reduce our group of friends to tearful laughter by using an accent or funny voice to order breakfast at a restaurant, pay for something at a store, or even to diffuse tension during a long rehearsal or writing session. As with any skill, some people are naturally gifted at character voices and some are not.

It isn't necessary, though, to be especially skilled at character voices to use them effectively in the classroom. None of us is in training to be the next Bart Simpson. If you wish to practice using character voices in the course of your lesson, there are a few techniques you can use to hone your skills. Pitch, rate, and volume are qualities of the voice which can be manipulated to develop character voices. Although not technically associated with the voice, the effective use of attitude, gesture, and posture are also critical to creating believable character voices.

These five techniques will help you create entertaining and believable characters in your classroom.

Pitch. Pitch refers to how high or low you place the notes in your voice. In other words, are you speaking in a high voice, a low voice, or somewhere in between? That explanation brings to mind the children's story of "Goldilocks and the Three Bears." If you were to develop voices for the main characters in this story, Baby Bear might have a high-pitched "baby" voice, while Papa Bear would most likely have a chest-rumbling basso-profoundo-style voice. Mama Bear and Goldilocks would be pitched somewhere between each other, Mama Bear lower to suggest that she is older than Baby Bear, with Goldilocks pitched high enough to emphasize her youth or femininity, perhaps. This is just one example of how a teacher could use pitch to breathe life into the character he or she is portraying.

Rate. Rate refers to how fast you are speaking. Are you speaking quickly, slowly, or at an average speed? Again, when the bears discover someone has been sleeping in their beds—*and she's still there!*—their rate of speech will increase to underscore their nervous energy. *Of Mice and Men*'s Lennie, on the other hand, who has more trouble organizing and structuring his thoughts, is going to speak at a more slow and carefully measured rate.

Volume. Volume refers to how loudly you are speaking. A brash, obnoxious character, obviously, will speak more loudly than a shy, reserved, or mysterious character. Jack, in *Lord of the Flies,* who lusts for power and is an arrogant bully who pushes people around will most likely be a louder speaker than Piggy, who serves as Jack's primary target and is portrayed as a hapless victim.

Attitude. Attitude refers to what personality, emotion, or disposition are you expressing through the use of your voice and body language. For example, the character voice you are using should allow room for you to suggest—through your vocal inflections—hints of any sadness, anger, frustration, longing, joy, or desire that the character may be feeling (for more on inflection, please see the previous chapter). By effectively using attitude in a reading, a skilled teacher could easily illustrate Jack's absolute disdain for Piggy and Piggy's abject fear of Jack in any given scene of *Lord of the Flies.*

Posture. Posture refers to the body language you use as you perform your character voice. As in real life, individual people stand or sit in individual ways, using individual mannerisms. This is a great way to differentiate between two characters. As a brief example, Goldilocks will simply stand differently than Papa Bear because of their gender, age, size, and lifestyle (not to mention species!). Using two distinct postures for two characters is like giving each character an individual fingerprint or "look" that students can use to identify who is speaking.

Gesture. Gesture refers to how a character uses his or her arms, hands, and fingers. My Italian relatives—characters in themselves—taught me the benefits of gesture early in life. They all spoke with their hands and every one of them had their signature movements. Uncle Leonard, when making a point, would touch his thumb to his ring finger and repeatedly shove his hand at you. When my grandfather disagreed with someone, he used to wave his hand away, as if dismissing the person completely. The gestures these people used were also as singular to them as fingerprints. A prepared teacher will add a few well-placed (and very distinctive) gestures to indicate an individual character. These gestures must not be random, however, but rather must spring naturally from the character's personality. They should give the listener insight into the characters' hearts and minds. As an example, our old friend Lennie, for whom thought is a confusing chore, might scratch his head a lot when he speaks. His mannerism springs directly from his personal lifestyle, personality, and individual circumstances. Use gestures that support the message in the text and clarify the identity of the characters.

These techniques cannot be used individually. While they can be practiced by themselves in a rehearsal situation, it is the *combination* of pitch, rate, volume, attitude, posture, and gesture that creates a credible character voice. One character may have a high, speedy, loud voice with a hostile attitude and a stiff posture. Another character might have more a low, slow, and quiet voice, with a sad attitude, and a slumped posture from fatigue or resignation. It depends, ultimately, on how each teacher interprets that character's personality. It is up to you, as the performer, to decide.

And remember: There are no wrong answers.

Character voices can be used sparingly or liberally, as necessitated by the lesson. They are also not just limited to use by teachers of literature. You can throw a single line into a lecture using a different, funny, sad, or angry voice just to emphasize an important point or merely to rouse those sleepy students in the back of the room. Similarly, one can work on developing entire characters for specific units, lessons, or concepts (a science teacher could consider using an extremely agitated, high-pitched, and speedy voice with a nervous attitude to bring to life the electron whizzing around the nucleus).

Other Forms of Character Voices

Original voices can also be created from scratch to create believable characters. Teachers can also do impressions of celebrities, politicians, or other famous or infamous people when it's time to tell anecdotes, stories, or jokes. I am reminded of the scene in *Dead Poet's Society* where Robin Williams performs Shakespeare as both John Wayne and Marlon Brando. Today we might imitate Clint Eastwood or Sylvester Stallone. Steal liberally and shamelessly from real life. Teachers can use character voices to mimic anyone from the President of the United States to the anchorperson on the local news. Character voices can spice up a lesson, make a class more lively and animated, and add levels of depth and meaning to your teaching performance style.

A science teacher I know, for example, uses the voices of Forrest Gump and Arnold Schwarzenegger (talk about a spectrum!) to make important points about biology, as well as what he calls his "whiny student" voice—most likely to discourage his own students from taking that approach with him regarding grades, deadlines, or assignments. Another social science teacher talked about how he used a "whispery voice" to do a satire of a Calvin Klein commercial, television ads that are known for their use of intimate vocalizations which are used to entice viewers to listen. These teachers have lifted voices from real-life people and events and added an extra dimension to their teaching styles—namely, that it is easier for their students to relate to the material because they have heard these voices in their own lives.

I have used characters voices in my own classroom with great success. As I mentioned previously, I use them frequently with *Of Mice and Men*, but they come in handy other times during the year as well. When teaching my juniors, for example, I always begin *The Catcher in the Rye* by reading chapter one aloud to them. It is my hope that by using an angry, disillusioned, teenage voice to introduce them to Holden Caulfield that Holden's voice will stick in their heads as they read and they relate more thoroughly to his emotions and experiences along his journey.

For most of the fiction I read aloud, I create voices I hope will bring the characters to life and make the reading interesting for the students. Other times, I do imitations of voices that come straight from the news, television, or movies. While teaching *The Great Gatsby* a few years ago, we were discussing the scene where Gatsby has invited Daisy over to his house and shows off his possessions by tossing on the bed all of his brand new shirts, some of which are still in the packages. As he does this, Daisy begins to cry softly.

I ask my students why Gatsby was throwing his shirts on the bed and why it made Daisy cry. Apparently, it was early enough in the morning that my students were still drowsy and therefore there was no response. It turned into one of those moments teachers dread where I had to answer my own question.

"He was showing her his stuff," I said, a little irritation growing into my voice. I'm starting to sound just like Jerry Seinfeld, I thought. So I told them.

"I'm starting to sound like Seinfeld."

They laughed in recognition, so I went into a nasal, slightly New York-ese accent, and imitated a rapid-fire exchange between some of the characters on Seinfeld's sit-com.

"He's showing her his stuff!"

"She's looking at all of his stuff!"

"Why should she care about his stuff?"

"What's with all that stufffffffffff?????"

By the end of my little scene, they were laughing and offering suggestions as to why Gatsby's shirts were important enough for him to show off and to move Daisy to tears. They'll remember that scene in the novel a lot longer because I associated it with a voice they knew from their own experience.

Remember, too: your students are *not* film critics. They are not going to critique your performance any more than they normally do. You don't have to be perfect. You just have to commit to a voice that makes your point and is comfortable to perform.

Not only will your students believe in the character you have created, but you may actually find the lesson more enjoyable yourself.

IMPROVISATION

16

IMPROVISATION

Teachers are improvisers.

We speak extemporaneously. Few, if any, of us have written scripts we memorize and perform. This is for the best. We should not be confined by a "canned" version of the message we wish to communicate. Learning is about spontaneity, liberation of minds, and experimentation. Teachers should have the freedom to follow a train of thought, even it leads to a dead end. A pre-scripted lesson would make this impossible.

The closest thing teachers have to a script might be a blueprint, lecture notes, or some kind of an outline. From these, teachers usually ad-lib their insights, instructions, and anecdotes. But teachers rarely take this act of improvisation to its next logical plateau. This next step, though, involves a deeper trust in improvisation and greater leap of faith.

Since most lessons involve some kind of overall objective, teachers frequently know exactly where they and their students will arrive by the end of the session. They know the ending of the story. But the truly inspired in our profession often explore areas where they aren't exactly certain where the road will lead or what souvenirs they might come back with when they return. They encourage the freedom of thought to explore subordinate or parallel thoughts without the certainty they will reap anything of value at all.

Comedians and musicians refer to this as "riffing." They frequently experiment within the structure of their performance to see what new material they can develop by just improvising on a certain subject, or in the case of the musician, a certain musical scale. (Think Robins Williams or Miles Davis). While learning how to riff effectively takes practice, more often than not, the performer comes back with something he or she didn't have before. A new guitar lick for the musician, perhaps, or a new joke for the comic, or in the case of the teacher, a new comparison, activity, insight, or anecdote. Teachers could learn something about ad-libbing and improvisation from observing comedians and musicians.

There are three requirements for successful improvisation in the classroom: 1) a comfortable environment, 2) a working atmosphere free of judgment or criticism, and 3) an unconditional acceptance of the improvisation motto: "Don't Deny!"

First of all, if students are given an environment where they are physically, mentally, and emotionally comfortable, they are more likely to explore and experiment with new concepts, ideas, and paradigms. Secondly, their exploration and experimentation have a better chance of teaching them something if they feel they will not be judged, criticized, or embarrassed for their choices, let alone for their successes and failures. And finally, in improvisational acting, no one has the right to deny what another person does in a scene. If two people are improvising a scene onstage, for example, and one person says, "How much for a loaf of marble rye?" indicating that the scene takes place in a New York bakery, the other person should not then say, "And boy these Louisiana jail cells surely do get warm this time of year," which would indicate they are actually incarcerated somewhere in the South. Actors use, and play off what their partners give them. In improvisation, denying what your partner has set up is deadly. And so it should be while improvising in the classroom. As a teacher, discuss at the outset what the appropriate parameters are for the lesson. Then allow any and all ideas come up and *accept them all*; see where they lead. Do not deny any of the ideas your students share. (one small caveat: this is not to suggest that I advocate the acceptance of the obscene, profane, or inappropriate). Have faith that they will know how far to go and what is enough. Similarly, do not allow your students to deny each other (e.g. "That's a stupid answer!").

Trust them; and give them the space to trust each other.

With improvisation, you never know exactly what to expect. This is both its joy and its risk. You may get to the end of the road and find nothing, but sometimes the trip itself is worth the effort. For obvious reasons, then, it takes a great deal of trust, faith, and confidence to riff with the best of them.

But the dividends can be astounding.

The excitement in improvisation is not knowing where things might lead, but knowing you have to go there anyway.

17

FREE ASSOCIATION

Imagine you are in a play. It's opening night, and you have butterflies in your stomach because your cue is coming up, but you step onstage despite the nervousness. Before you know it, the scene is going very smoothly. The rhythm and timing are good, the communication between you and your partner is electric. Suddenly, your partner forgets his line and stands there, dumbfounded, staring at you with a stricken look on his face.

What do you do?

What if you can't just skip to the next line because what he was supposed to say was a pivotal plot point?

What then?

Every actor on the planet has been on both sides of this situation. When it happens, performers must think quickly and improvise in such a way that informs the actors where to go and what to say next, while still including all the information necessary to advance the plot. As the old saying goes, the show must go on.

Not an easy task.

The answer is free association. Actors learn to improvise by free associating in tight spots like the one mentioned above. They start with the general idea their characters were speaking about and then jump to the most closely related idea or bit of information. The objective is to link the other performers back to a spot where everyone can pick up the thread of the memorized lines and the blocking set in rehearsal by the director.

Free associating, then, does not refer to the cliché of the psychologist saying, "A rolling stone..." and the couched patient having to choose quickly between, "gathers no moss" and "shouldn't tour after the age of fifty." Rather, free associating—as it impacts education—refers to spontaneously jumping from idea to idea to see where they will lead and exploring their connections and relationships. Free association can help a teacher identify, illuminate, and work within patterns that exist in the concepts she is teaching.

The concept of free association can be as important in the classroom as it is on the boards. Secondary teachers can use free association to create some wonderfully meaningful moments in their classrooms. Middle and high school students are at a point in their intellectual development where they are intrigued with abstract concepts and enjoy making connections between disparate ideas. On the other hand, this also means they are equally fond of seeing what road they can get the teacher to go down by doing a little free associating themselves. Teachers may find themselves beginning a class discussion on setting in Steinbeck's *The Red Pony* and ending it on the horsepower in the '65 Ford Mustang. As far as the students are concerned, they're still on topic because they're still talking about horses. For this reason, it is important that your attempts at free association do not become rambling dissertations that have nothing to do with the goals or objectives of the prepared lesson (educators refer to these digressions—sneeringly—as "birdwalks").

Free association is best used within the confines of a structured lecture, lesson plan, or discussion. Again, if you've ever seen Robin Williams perform, you've witnessed the master of free association as he "riffs" within a structured lesson (or, in his case, comedy routine). For the computer-minded, free associating might be akin to "linking" from one website to another while on The Internet.

In the classroom, one "links" from idea to idea.

This method of improvisation, however, should not be used as an excuse to skip developing detailed and specific lesson plans. Only an irresponsible and unprofessional teacher would arrive in the classroom unprepared and without a plan, happily declaring, "I'm just going to 'free associate' my whole lesson today!" However, if you are in the middle of a lecture and the math problem, or period of history, or novel chapter reminds you of your great aunt's biceps, don't be afraid to make the leap as long as you've also made the instantaneous judgment call that the leap will further clarify the issue at hand.

Do free associations always hit paydirt? Of course not. I've explored ideas I felt were related to my lesson and driven them right into brick walls. On the other hand, free association has been responsible for some wonderful—and wonderfully educational—moments. And when that happens, you have created a unique moment of learning in your classroom that will occur only for your students and only at that moment in time. The ephemeral nature of free association when used in a lesson plan makes this experience just about the closest teaching becomes to live theater.

Your students see a one-of-a-kind performance every time!

Once, for instance, we were studying William Carlos Williams as part of my junior poetry unit. I knew I wanted my students to do an original poem copying the form (and opening line) of Williams' poem, "The Red Wheelbarrow" ("So much depends upon…") While I would suggest that a teacher always have a model handy, I felt that, in this case, creating one ahead of time would be artificial, and I wanted the example to be fresh, immediate, and with luck, one they could relate to. I did not think anything I came up with in advance would help them as much as creating one on the spot using my immediate circumstances as inspiration. Enjoying both improvisation and poetry as much as I do, free association became an easier and more exciting option for me as the teacher.

As I began the poem model, I really had no idea where I was going, but I had faith that something would reveal itself to me. Then I saw Steve sitting in the front row, looking up expectantly. Steve was a star player on the varsity basketball team. He had been enjoying the class, but was not its strongest writer. He was improving, though, and I instantly realized how I could connect him to the world of poetry in a way that might make a lasting impression. In a world where most students—boys, especially—come to class harboring primarily negative responses to poetry ("This is sissy stuff!"), I saw a small window of opportunity to enlighten Steve in the joys of poetic language. I looked directly at him, gesture toward him to show everyone he was about to be the star of my poem, and improvised the following:

> So much depends upon
> that last free throw
>
> whizzing through
> the basket,
>
> seconds before
> the buzzer
>
> nothing
> but net.

Both the smile on his face and the light I saw go on in his head told me he'd made a connection with the model and that he was happy to have been made a part of the process. Free association works best when you are alert to your environment and can use information that is close at hand.

Steve was in first period. Instead of coming up with a whole new model for second period, I simply modified the model to fit my new environment. While my students wrote dutifully in their journals during the beginning of class, I looked around the room and found Michael, another varsity basketball player. When the time came for the model, I did the same thing (established eye contact, gestured in Michael's direction, recited the model). To the students, it seemed as if I had, at a moment's notice, chosen someone in the room as an instant example and worked him into the lesson. Certainly that had been more accurate in period one, but all I had to do during second period was free associate using the basketball idea and find the appropriate element of the new environment (in this case, Michael) to complete my message. In short, I needed a new *basketball player*, not a new *example*.

When free associating:

- Be alert to your environment

- Link only to related ideas for the purposes of clarification

- Free associate only within a structure

- Encourage students to also free associate within the structure of the lesson

- Keep ideas linked to the subject matter

Remember that not all leaps to related ideas, not matter how brilliant the split-second inspiration, are going to work perfectly. That's all right. Sometimes we have to know which ideas won't work to guide us in the direction of those that will.

Learning, at its most fundamental, is about exploration. Teachers must feel free to explore the subject matter in a way that allows each individual to learn based on his or her personal needs. Teachers must be courageous enough to risk going in the wrong direction because, really, what are a few U-turns on the way to enlightenment?

18

TRUST

We all remember times when our trust in someone has been betrayed. It is not a good feeling. The dictionary refers to trust as, "The confident expectation of something." This definition creates an all-encompassing picture of how trust can function between two people. If you trust another person, you have a confident expectation he or she will not insult, betray, hurt, embarrass, disappoint, humiliate, or otherwise undermine the positive emotional bond inherent in your relationship.

Trust, therefore, is a powerful tool in any situation involving two or more people. Every relationship—from business to friendship to marriage—benefits from a foundation of trustworthiness and respect.

Trust binds relationships together.

Actors are big on trust. Actors trust each other not to forget their lines, hurt their fellow actors during scenes of passion or violence, or criticize highly-stylized or experimental performance choices. When actors do not trust each other a sense of fear, dread, or suspicion can interrupt the flow of communication onstage and sabotage performances, sometimes even entire productions. They trust each other to come to each performance prepared and focused on the work before them—and usually this works. It is a truism in the theater that the more trust there is between actors, the better the performance because anything is possible.

Trust also plays a vital role in the functioning of a successful classroom. Both students and teacher must feel they can trust each other so that everyone's energy is focused on learning. There are three types of trust in the classroom: Trust between student and teacher, trust between students, and trust in one's self.

Trust Between Student and Teacher

Trust between student and teacher is of paramount importance; it is what bonds instructor and learner. Nothing will impair the learning environment more than when one of these two parties betrays the trust of the other. Trust between student and teacher is the epitome of *the confident expectation of something*. The teacher has a confident expectation that the student will come to class prepared, respectful, and ready to learn. Furthermore, he or she trusts that the student will satisfy this and other set expectations. The student, conversely, has the confident expectation that the teacher will be knowledgeable, helpful, and also respectful. Students trust that teachers, who are usually the wiser and more mature of the two, will not abuse the power and authority they possess.

Nothing will break the trust a student has in a teacher faster than if that teacher does not respect the student as a person. Similarly, nothing will break respect for a teacher faster than if that teacher breaks the trust the student has developed.

I value the trust my students place in me. Over the years, many students have confided in me their most guarded secrets; everything from problems at home to crushes they have on other students. They share these stories with me because they trust that I will respect their feelings. I have been happy to be, on occasion, a counselor, friend, advisor, and sounding board. Many of these students have no one else to whom they can turn.

The trust my students place in me means a lot to me, and I guard it vigilantly because I feel it makes me not only a better teacher, but a better human being. They know that even if their work or behavior is not completely up to par, that I will not embarrass, humiliate, or criticize them. I will make every effort to let them know I'm on their side and that we need to find a solution together. These remediations should never be made publicly. Similarly, there is no trust builder in the classroom as powerful as a teacher's ability—when necessary—to make a sincere, swift, and heartfelt apology. These apologies should *often* be made publicly.

Trust Between Students

When I taught drama classes, it was imperative that I set up a non-judgmental atmosphere for novice actors to explore their talent. In a creative environment such as drama, it is crucial for students to feel they can experiment without criticism, humiliation, or embarrassment. They must trust that everything doesn't have to work perfectly, and that they can try things that fail. This won't be the case, however, if they are trying to be creative, but fear that other students may tease or make fun of them or their performance choices. This lack of trust will paralyze their learning and growth as both students and performers.

If the drama teacher is teaching about physicality, for example, and has instructed the class to walk around the classroom as if they are up to their knees in peanut butter (or ping pong balls or feathers, or whatever), everyone knows how silly this is going to look and knows they must be able to trust their fellow actors not to point fingers and laugh. There is also usually a great sense of togetherness in these classes which helps everyone learn to work together without making negative judgments about one another's performances.

For this reason, drama students tend to develop faster and deeper relationships in their drama classes than in many other subject areas because they are forced to trust and rely on each other so intensively in their training that, when they emerge from the drama program, many have become friends for life.

All students, not just those pursuing acting, deserve a supportive atmosphere in which to work, but it was a small revelation to me to realize that a creative environment without judgment could work well in any subject area. Shortly after, I incorporated this concept—with powerful results—into each of my English classes.

If a student reads aloud or gives a presentation or even speaks during a class discussion, I consider it a performance and admonish the class to, "Be a good audience," a line I've stolen directly from my drama classes. Knowing the reading or presentation will not be judged or criticized, the performing student is more able to relax and reach is or her potential. Creating this same sense of acceptance works just as well during class discussions, where students will feel they can contribute personal viewpoints without fear of reprisal or censure by either the teacher or the other students.

Trust between students is a keystone for any classroom where learning takes place. Our goals as teachers should be to make all learning environments creative, non-judgmental, and trusting.

Trust in Oneself

In 1988, I was cast in a small role in the daytime drama, *General Hospital.*

I had one line.

The soap opera process works very quickly. You come in, do your part, and say good-bye. There's a better than average chance that you will never see anyone connected to the show again in your natural life. It's the acting equivalent of the automobile assembly line. There was a brief rehearsal, a tremendous amount of down time for me personally while they shot other scenes (in other words, lots of time for fear and anxiety and self-doubt to set in), and finally we shot the scene.

When I was called to the set, I walked bravely to the spot where, during rehearsal, the director said I should stand. He then busied himself with setting up the other actors, went back to his chair, and set up the shot with the camera operator. After what seemed an eternity, we heard the proverbial, "quiet on the set" and, finally, the director called, "Action."

The scene took a whopping sixty seconds to shoot. I waited for the other actors to cross the set, say their lines, and right before my cue, I crossed to my new spot and uttered my single, "unforgettable" line.

The leading lady in the cast had one more line, then the director yelled, "Cut!"

The cast and crew immediately burst into a riot of explosive laughter.

I was convinced I had absolutely blown the scene. In that instant, I was sure I had done something horrible, so unfixable, that all they could do was laugh hysterically that anyone would let this no-talent hack through the stage door. I was certain it would be my last experience in what pro ballplayers affectionately call "The Show."

In my arrogance, I thought the scene would, of course, need to be redone because of my horrendous gaff. Suddenly, though, the director called, "Next shot!" and everyone forgot I was there, except for a stagehand who knew it was my virgin experience in professional show business and came over and said to me, "Good job."

I never did find out why they were laughing.

I was amazed when I saw the show on television a month later. I knew how I felt inside while the cameras were rolling (in my nervousness, my ears roared with the sound of the ocean; I could barely hear the other actors saying their lines), but no one would ever know that from watching the scene. I was never going to give Al Pacino a run for his money, but I looked poised, self-assured, and relatively natural. Most importantly, I looked like I belonged right where I was, doing what I was doing.

My experience on *General Hospital* taught me that not only do we have to trust ourselves as professionals, but we must learn to trust our training. It will be there for us when we need it.

As teachers, we've trained for years in the best methods to maximize student learning and beginning teachers frequently walk into the classroom as petrified as I was walking onto the *GH* set. I spent over a decade learning to act, and when it came down to it, my technique came through for me. That day, I learned I could always trust that my acting skills would be there for me when I needed them.

Teachers can trust that they are professionals and deserve the respect and prestige their jobs have to offer, and that the methods they've learned and practiced over the years will serve them when they are feeling less than confident.

Without trust in oneself, it's very difficult to develop any other kind of trust at all.

PERFORMANCE

19

STRUCTURE

Structure is the blueprint for any performance. It is the playwright's job, for instance, to make certain the text has structure through such conventions as act and scene breaks, conflict and resolution, and endings. It is the director's job to make certain the performance has structure through tension, pacing, stage composition (how actors are arranged on the stage in their blocking to present a pleasing "picture"), and comic relief. Furthermore, it is the actor's responsibility to make certain each characterization has structure through his or her use of such acting strategies as rhythm, analysis, delivery, and finally, transformation (how a character changes during the course of the storyline). Even the audience helps a production maintain its structure through such simple behaviors as observing the intermission timelines and knowing when to laugh, applaud, and when to be silent. These elements punctuate a performance—adding, as it were, commas, periods, exclamation points, question marks—incorporating a series of little beats throughout the show that ultimately help order and organize the events as they occur on-stage.

Without structure, theatrical performances would be anarchy. Imagine a play where the first act is an hour and a half, but the second act is a mere ten minutes. Even worse, picture an audience that ignores the curtain time and arrives individually and at will, talks during performances, and yells at the performers as they perform. We've all attended performances, of course, where one or two people have done these things, but if audiences behaved this way on a grander scale, there would be theatrical bedlam.

In the classroom, it is the teacher's job—one of the sacred missions of the profession, if you ask me—to make certain the lesson plan has structure and that students are not subjected to a lesson whose first act is an hour and a half and the second act, ten minutes. There should be signposts along the way to indicate where we've been, where we are, and where we are going. Consequently, the following concepts of structure work as well in the classroom as they do onstage.

Don't Ramble

The first law of structure in teaching is Don't Ramble.

My seventh grade social studies teacher, Mr. Smitrovich (not his real name), rambled incessantly. Many days the bell would ring and he would launch into period-long monologues that meandered near and around the subject of social studies, but never explored, explicated, or explained the subject. If veering off the topic of the lecture material is "birdwalking," Mr. Smitrovich was the John Audubon of Prospect Avenue School.

When teachers ramble, they not only neglect their subject area; they neglect their students. They deprive students of the very information they deserve. Certainly teachers must learn to use anecdotal and story-telling devices in their lecture style to keep it lively and engaging, but those stories and anecdotes should be well-paced and tightly structured and, of course, be relevant to whatever information is being taught at the moment. These personal tidbits must illuminate the point being made, not sidestep it.

Mr. Smitrovich, on the other hand, spent days telling us about his days on the farm or whatever he was reminiscing about at the moment. We learned very little about social studies that year. I can't tell you about the topography of Spain, but I do know far too much about Mr. Smitrovich's messy divorce.

Teachers should either know where they are going in their material or make it a conscious decision to improvise with the subject or information. Directionless lecture is one of the worst possible teaching techniques, performance-centered or otherwise.

Relationships

Teachers are constantly looking for relationships between elements of their subject matter and are constantly trying to make those connections clear to their students. They either want to identify a relationship (or connection) between two concepts or between the concept and the students' personal experience. English teachers, for example, look for the relationships between friendship and loneliness in *Of Mice and Men* or the connections between the Salem witchhunts as dramatized in *The Crucible* and the McCarthy hearings of the 1950's.

As a rule, high school teachers are on a constant search for patterns that will clarify literature for young readers. Math teachers look for relationships between numbers, science teachers look for connections between chemicals and physical laws, and physical education teachers might look for the connection between physiology and athletic prowess.

Frequently, however, teachers design lessons that miss out on one of the most basic—and easily constructed—relationships of all: beginnings, middles, and ends.

When a teacher is not careful to structure a lesson with a clear beginning, middle, and end, students can become disoriented and confused long before any ideas have a chance to be communicated. Without a clear beginning, for example, students may have no idea the teacher has even introduced a new unit, lesson, or idea. Without a clear middle, students may not realize a teacher has made a transition into related material. Finally, without a clear ending, students may be confused as to how one lesson connects with another or where an idea falls in sequence.

Sometimes students will find the relationships and connections for you.

I was about to teach *The Great Gatsby* one year and I usually introduce the novel by showing what was currently happening in the world of poetry during the 1920's. I brought in some of e.e. cummings poems, including one called, "my sweet old etc." In this poem, a young man is overseas during wartime (World War I, one assumes) and writes home to his wife or girlfriend. He discusses rather mundane issues of home, family, and relatives, but in his haste—we get the feeling he is close to the front—he must use the word "etc." frequently to indicate things he either cannot or does not want to say. The very last "etc." is used somewhat suggestively. To wit:

"(dreaming/et cetera, of/Your smile/eyes knees and of your Etcetera)."

The class usually gets a kick out of this slightly bawdy reference, and I explain how—unlike today—writers had to be very clever about when they wrote about certain, less-than-appropriate topics. A few units later, we were reading Salinger's *The Catcher in the Rye,* and I was trying to explain why Holden Caulfield was so upset with his roommate Stradlater. Stradlater, who is one of the private school's star jocks and best known womanizers, has a date with Jane Gallagher, a girl Holden used to know and on whom he still has a crush. Holden goes on and on about how nice and sweet Jane is and how he is immensely troubled to think that Stradlater is only interested in trying to, as he puts it, "give her the time." I said to the class, "Holden is interested in Jane's mind, while Stradlater is interested in…"

And Sonia, a girl in the front row, yelled out, "her et cetera."

Teachers should locate and illuminate relationships between concepts. Don't be afraid, however, to let your students help you locate them for you.

Storytelling

Everybody loves a good story. From the time we are children, we hear tales that entertain us, inform us, and educate us. We learned the difference between right and wrong via fairytales and the models for correct behavior from good friends like Captain Kangaroo or Mr. Rogers.

Stories can also be used in the classroom to teach us subject content.

Teachers should learn to spin a good yarn because students love to hear them. Teachers can use both true, personal anecdotes and fictional stories to create interesting patterns and vivid images for their students. Stories can be used in the classroom both as a form of introducing new information or enriching existing knowledge. This is true not only in English or literature class, but in any other subject as well.

The science teacher can talk about her experience working on an oil pipeline in Alaska. The math teacher can write a narrative in code that students break and rewrite by solving equations. The band teacher can tell of his escapades—some of them, anyway—wearing the polyester leisure suit and playing the synthesizer in that disco band in 1978. Each of us has a million experiences we can draw on to clarify subject matter for our students.

Students love when I tell them about the night I attended the MTV Video Music Awards and sat next to Cher and Madonna, or the time I was hired to play one of twenty life-sized toy soldiers at a private Christmas party at an oil baron's mansion in Beverly Hills. I use the MTV story when teaching the personal essay (Topic: What was one of the most exciting nights of your life?) and the toy soldier story when teaching *The Great Gatsby*, a story of people so rich they take others for granted (Discussion topic: How much money is too much money? Well class, I say, there was a time when I met a man who had so much money he could hire human beings as decorations for his party! Now *that's* a lot of money).

The opportunities to use stories in the classroom are endless.

They are also a fun way to learn.

Teachers must keep in mind that even if they have told a certain story a hundred times, the students sitting in front of them this year have never heard it. Therefore, they must tell it as if it is the first time. The story should carry a sense of enthusiasm, mystery, and wonder that all stories have the first time we hear them.

In *Audition*, author Michael Shurtleff writes that when performers tell a story, they must begin at "the point of innocence." He says:

"We create reality by telling the story in the same sequence it happened to us, that is, we start at a point of innocence, the point where we were innocent of what was going to happen and thought it was going to be a day or night like any other" (151).

Shurtleff gives an example of telling a story of leaving a class for the night, walking to a car, seeing a man, and the man pulls out a knife…Shurtleff wisely points out that, if you wish to create suspense in your story, you would never start that story by saying, "A man pulled a knife on me last night." By not telling the end of the story first, Shurtleff says, we create suspense and mystery. Relating the story in the same sequence it happened, on the other hand, allows us to recreate the intensity and reality of the situation for the listener.

When telling a story in the classroom, I follow Shurtleff's advice. Beginning from a point where my audience is innocent of what is going to happen, I not only create suspense and reality, but good drama which, it is my hope, keeps my students engaged and interested.

Another thing to keep in mind when telling stories is to imbue each story with a sense of spontaneity and immediacy. An old comic friend of mine once shared this advice: "Tell every *new* joke as if you've told it a million times and tell every *old* joke as if it's the first time you've ever told it." This means that an audience wants to watch a confident performer, regardless of the performer's confidence in the material itself. If everything you relate to your audience can walk the fine tightrope of sounding new and fresh as well as tried and true, it will be easier for you as the performer to gain their trust and attention. If you apply this advice to storytelling in the classroom, each story you tell will be fresh, original, and spontaneous.

Suspense

One element of a good story is suspense. A good story makes us wonder what is going to happen next. A story that has suspense can "hook" us more easily and cause us to keep reading or watching.

Good teachers create suspense in their lesson plans. They structure the lesson in a way that causes the student to want to know what happens next. There are as many ways to create suspense as there are lesson plans.

Let the structure fit the subject matter, idea, or unit.

One method I frequently use to create a sense of anticipation in my students is the cliffhanger. This method is as old as The Perils of Pauline (I learned it, however, from the campy 60's TV show *Batman*). I let the lesson get to its most intense moment, and then I stop the action and move on to something else. The students frequently groan, whine, and complain for me to keep going, but I do not listen. Whenever we pick up from that point again, usually the next day, the students are rapt, wondering what is going to happen next. Films, obviously, are a great place to use the cliffhanger technique because the suspense is already built in. Let the story build to just near a climax in the plotline and then hit the "STOP" button on the VCR.

I use it frequently, too, for pieces of literature.

While reading *The Crucible,* I will stop right after John Proctor tears up the confession he has signed and right before he hangs for allegedly being a warlock. I have even been known to say, as a bit of foreshadowing and for my own amusement, "Gee, I'm sorry to keep you hanging, but that's where we need to stop for the day."

The key to suspense is the placement of the details and beats. In other words, place the most important concept as close to the end of the lesson or discussion or assignment as possible to increase suspense, anticipation, and intrigue. This will also work for the most significant point you are making or the most intense moment of the lesson you have planned. Place the most critical information at the end, and create a sense of urgency and suspense and, just like watching a good movie or reading a good novel, students will be anxious to reach the end of the "story," and to find out what happens next.

Tension

In the first section of this book, I talked about how to eliminate the ugly specter of tension from your daily teaching style. I emphasized the importance of relaxation and the absence of anxiety to ensure an optimum performance in the classroom. Certain types of tension, however, can be positive; they can take an average lesson plan and make it superior.

Using physical tension to your advantage, for instance, can improve the electricity in a lesson. During intense moments in a lesson, keep your muscles taut as you teach—almost as if you were about to play a sport; as if you were a short stop and you were waiting for the batter to pop one just to the left of the pitcher's mound—right to you. One of the best (and easiest) times to use physical tension to create an intense moment of teaching is in the use of imaginary objects (see chapter 29).

If you were holding a sword, for example, your arm muscles would tense in the places where you needed to support the weight of the sword. The same is true if you were picking up an apple. Tense your muscles where they would tense to support the weight of the object and the intensity of the physical tension will transfer to your audience. Result: they will play closer attention. In short, the use of appropriate physical tension will make your gestures seem more dynamic and realistic.

Students will pick up on your physical tension, and it will create a sense of anticipation and importance in them (i.e., this *must* be important, they might think, because that guy's wound as tight as a spring!). The right type of physical tension in the can—like emotional tension in a good story—keep the listeners engaged, on the edge of their seats, and in suspense.

A good lesson is built like a good story. And all effective story structure contains elements of tension as a means of keeping the listener's (or reader's) attention. Leading your students to believe that anything could happen next (or that you could say or do anything) creates a positive type of tension that keeps them involved and interested in what's happening. Creating cliffhangers at the end of lessons, class periods, or units and using the benefits of physical tension keep them coming back for more.

Conflict and Resolution

All stories, whether in the guise of novels, plays, short stories, television shows, or movies, have conflict and resolution. Characters want something and are faced with problems or obstacles that prevent them from getting it. The interest in the story is generated from the audience wanting to know how the characters fare while faced with this conflict (Does the boy get the girl? Does the detective find the killer? Does the poor farmer save his land before the bank forecloses? etc.). Good stories usually tell us, sometime before they end, whether or not the characters were able to reach the goal or overcome the obstacles to get what they want. This sense of resolution and closure is very satisfying to the audience and, therefore, makes them want to read another novel, see another movie, or watch another television show.

Conflict and resolution is an easy structural device to use effectively in the classroom. Science and math are prime examples. The teacher states a math problem or a science teacher sets up a hypothesis to an experiment (conflict), which creates a sense of suspense in the student (they want to know if the conflict will be resolved or the mystery solved or what the result of the experiment is) and then, sometime before the end of the lesson, either the teacher or they themselves should have come up with an answer to the math problem or have discovered the results of the experiment. Once the students have that satisfying sense of resolution, they are more likely to want to follow the same procedure again, and thus more likely to want to follow the teacher wherever he or she goes next.

Introducing the concept of conflict and resolution into a lesson is very simple. There are two steps. First, the teacher must present a problem or conflict or question (or a classroom situation where there is a significant obstacle). Next, either the teacher must take steps to solve the problem or overcome the obstacle—which, by the way, can be philosophical or conceptual as well—or create an environment whereby students can.

Without structure, lesson plans either short change the ideas they attempt to present by ending too abruptly or smother them by going on and on with no real direction. Using elements like relationships, positive tension, storytelling, suspense, and conflict and resolution, your lesson will have an outline, a guide, an architecture that will help to give it shape and support. This will allow them to serve as a roadmap for the subject matter—not only for your students, but you as well.

20

PACING

Much like my junior high school experience with Mr. Smitrovich, we've all had that teacher who spends three days telling his class every gory and minute detail of his recent gall bladder surgery, only to find he has a piddly ten minutes left to discuss the many uses of a variable or the importance of the F-stop in photography. None of us, all things considered, learned very much from these teachers. We may have liked these teachers as people, enjoyed their little "birdwalks," or even thought how "cool" they were, but we walked out of their classrooms with precious little knowledge.

Other teachers would drone on for hour after hour, day after day, giving us no particular signal as to which were the important ideas and which were the subordinate ideas. They never adjusted their speed, never varied their routine, never emphasized or de-emphasized. We dreaded going to these classes because they were boring. They were all the same and all went at the same speed: slow. We emerged from these classes like zombies, our minds dulled and our senses numbed.

The two types of teachers mentioned above were very poor at pacing their classes to correspond with the material they were teaching. Pacing refers to how teachers organize and budget their time based on the amount of information they must communicate. It's timing the lesson plan to make the more important sections count more and carry more weight. Pacing helps the teacher in allowing the critical information in the lesson or unit stand out and, conversely, the less significant sections to breeze past. The way in which teachers pace their units, lectures, or lessons tells the students where the emphasis should be placed (and one would hope that the emphasis would be placed on the symbolism of the novel and the mathematical concept, and *not* the gall bladder surgery). The more time a teacher spends on any one particular issue or concept, the more important the student is likely to think that concept is; ergo, he or she is more likely to remember it. In short, proper pacing helps the student to know what to take notes on, what to study, and what to remember for the rest of his or her life.

Novelists are great at pacing. They often gloss over decades or centuries in two or three sentences. Consider these examples: "During the next generation, the Monroe family prospered," or, "Ten years later, Tom and Pamela divorced," or, "Only two months after the wedding, Marsha started showing." These phrases move the reader forward in time or significance, without stopping to cover unimportant details. Conversely, writers will slow down the narrative and give entire scenes, pages, or chapters over to an afternoon in a character's life if something monumental or pivotal is about to happen in that character's life or in the plotline of the novel. Many times entire chapters are devoted to one phone call or a serious conversation over dinner. Think of each class, then, as a chapter in the novel of your curriculum and pace it according to the significance of the events in the plotline.

In theater, there is very little latitude for the slow and boring. Playwrights who write poorly-paced scripts rarely see their work onstage and are forced into early retirement. Actors who do not learn the nuances of pacing end up languishing on soap operas and infomercials. Every book on the subject of acting has something to say about pacing, and yet almost no teacher education textbooks mention it. In *Audition*, author Michael Shurtleff writes an entire chapter about pacing...which is only two lines long. It says in its entirety: "Almost every reading I see is too slow. I have never seen a reading that is too fast."

Learn from the novelist. Learn from the theater. Learn from the teacher with bad pacing.

Not every lesson necessarily lends itself to *quick* pacing, however. Your job is to find the elements that need to be emphasized and place them in strategic places which will focus attention on them without unnecessarily slowing down the lesson. You must also leave out any extraneous information. Any activity or discussion that is not leading the class toward the objective of the lesson is irrelevant and should be left out, as it is an enemy to pace.

How do you achieve good pacing in the classroom? As with most good teaching, good pacing begins with planning. Structuring a yearly overview is the first step, the second is to break the year into the separate grading periods, then sketch out weekly plans and, finally, the daily lesson plans. This approach adds up to a well-organized, tightly paced curriculum.

Good pacing is also the result of action. Too many actions and the pace is too swift and hard to follow. Too few and the structure of the lesson disintegrates and the lesson falls apart and the objective is not met. A well-paced lesson will have its own momentum and direction, but will not have speed simply for speed's sake. Much like an actor imbues a monologue with a sense of urgency, a good lesson should have that same sense of urgency, as if the information being passed along is critical. This increases interest and effort on the part of the students. The well-paced lesson also has a sense of advancing the story, if you will, of *heading somewhere* (namely, toward the objective).

Teachers pay perilously little attention to pacing. Working with a captive audience, they don't always consider how interested their audience is or, perhaps, don't think that, just maybe, they are boring their listeners to death. The students are more likely to retain information—and therefore get a superior education—from a teacher who is sensitive to the pacing of his or her lesson. Teachers should take a lesson from Goldilocks and the Three Bears: Not too fast, not too slow, but just right.

Pace yourself.

21

EMOTION

Emotions are the actor's currency. Feelings are what actors trade in. A performance without emotion is pale, flat, and uninteresting. The audience is left with the feeling that if the actor does not care enough to generate any genuine feeling onstage, why should we make the effort to generate any feelings in the house? Good actors not only feel genuine emotion onstage, but train and condition as strenuously as ballerinas or gymnasts in methods which will effectively communicate those feelings to the audience.

A lot of effort in our society is spent teaching people that, where their jobs are concerned, personal feelings should be left at the door. While I do see the wisdom in that—outbursts full of personal issues and emotional baggage are hardly beneficial in most business or professional situations—it is necessary at times to communicate how we are feeling in a given situation. Teachers frequently feel they cannot let what happens in the classroom affect them or, if it does, they certainly feel like they must keep these feelings to themselves.

In actuality, the expression of a large array of controlled emotions is absolutely acceptable in the classroom. Teachers should learn to use emotions in the classroom to reinforce what they are teaching, to make lessons dynamic and dramatic, and to add mystery or intrigue.

This does takes practice, however.

In my first year of teaching, a class made me so angry one day I yelled at them. Immediately, I was overcome with shame and guilt for having yelled at the very young people who had been entrusted to my care. I felt as if I had mistreated them. On the way out of school that day, I ran into my supervisor.

"How are things going?" she asked.

"Fine," I said, my expression betraying my own inner emotions.

"What's wrong?" she said.

"Sixth period," I began, "made me so angry today that I yelled at them, and now I feel bad about it, like I shouldn't have."

"Why do you feel you shouldn't have yelled at them?"

"In college," I explained, "a professor taught us that, to be good teachers, we needed to love our subjects, love ourselves, and love our students."

"That sounds like a great approach," she said.

"I don't feel like I was showing my students that by yelling at them," I said.

"Sometimes," she said, "we show them we love them *by* yelling at them. Sometimes they need to know they're making us angry and that their behavior is affecting us, affecting our emotions."

Over the course of the year, we did, naturally, discuss more effective methods of showing students they are making us angry besides yelling, but my supervisor's sensitive listening and wisdom that day has always stayed with me. It is acceptable for teachers to share their emotions with their students. They will benefit not only from knowing *that* you feel, but by knowing *how* you feel.

There are exceptions to this approach, however.

During a journalism class I took at San Diego State University, a guest lecturer came and told us about his experiences as a reporter during the Watts riots during the 60's. His daughter was in the drama program with me, and it became immediately clear where she got her proclivity for performing. This man raced around the room, using anything handy to advance his story, sometimes even grabbing members of the audience and shaking them to make this point. He filled our class, much of the hallway, and parts of several other classrooms with the sound of his booming voice—a voice racked with emotion.

I happened to be sitting up front. Aside from being in a prime spot to be plucked from the audience and used as a player in his little one-man show, the level of emotion was so overpowering that I became embarrassed sitting there as if all the attention was being drawn to me. Some might say at least I remember the lecture, but I don't. I just remember the feelings of discomfort. My recollections of this speaker, while vivid, are far from positive.

This reporter-cum-performer exhibited too much emotion in the classroom. He did not know his audience (or playing area, for that matter). He gauged his performance too large for the room and for the group to which he was playing. His voice was too loud, his emotions were too large and intense, and his passion for his topic was over-whelming. He knew emotions could be a powerful teaching tool in the classroom—that they could move and touch a group of people—but it was like using a chainsaw to cut a dinner steak.

Not every class, of course, must become an encounter session where teachers vent their deepest fears, explore their most pointed insecuri-ties, or articulate their wildest fantasies. Using emotions in the class-room really is as simple as being comfortable enough to laugh when a student says something funny or to not be afraid to get a little choked up if something moves you (as I did the first few times I read the end-ing to *Of Mice and Men* aloud to my students). Similarly, if something bewilders or confuses you, feel free to tell them. If you are joyous or scared or angry about something, express that as well.

If the literature or concept or current event you are teaching infuri-ates you for some reason, raise your voice. Use your hands. Show the students the full range for your expression. They will not only accept it, they will learn from it. They will also learn models for responsible behavior when you give them a sense of your anger or hostility and they watch as you suppress it or control it because to vent it or release it unchecked would be unprofessional and inappropriate. As a rule, do not be afraid to show students what you are feeling. If enough trust has built up between your students and you, they will respect your feelings the same way you respect theirs.

Emotions are okay in the classroom.

They make you human.

22

ENVIRONMENT

Once I attended a play in a poorly designed theater. Two concrete poles, serving as the structural support of the building, were jutting up from the floor in the middle of the house, blocking entirely the onstage action of the play from several members of the audience. My lucky ticket entitled me to a seat directly behind one of these large pillars. Needless to say, I do not remember the name of the play or anything about the content or quality of the production. I had a lovely evening identifying geometrical shapes and small mythical animals in the stucco of the pole, but my play-going experience was ultimately ruined because of the necessary and unchangeable requirements of the physical structure in which the play took place. No matter how talented and graceful the actors were, or how moving or brilliant the text of the play, I could not see or hear what was happening, and this destroyed the entire theatrical experience.

Many classrooms suffer similar fates. A positive and pleasant environment is an intregal element of teaching success. Just like an audience needs a good theater structure to reap the benefits of an excellent stage production, students need—and deserve—to learn in a physical facility that is solidly built, pleasantly arranged both by architect and teacher), and well-lighted and ventilated.

The truth is that there are many aspects of physical structure that a teacher cannot change (much like the theater management could not remove the aforementioned pillars, lest the theater walls come tumbling down!). There a number of elements of environment, though, that the teacher *can* use to his or her advantage or manipulate to improve the learning curve of the class. Two of the easiest to use to your advantage are sightlines and walls.

Sightlines

In theater, whether or not the audience can clearly see the performers onstage is referred to as the audience's "sightlines." Directors check sightlines by sitting in various seats in the house to make sure every audience member can clearly view the stage composition the director is working so arduously to create.

Teachers should think of their students as audience members who must be able to see the onstage action and, therefore, to consider their students' sightlines from their desks.

For years, my desks were arranged in very orderly rows. As I mentioned in the chapter on "blocking," by arranging my desks in three sections around my room (it resembles a square horseshoe), I increased the "playing area" for the teacher, and I opened up the environment for my audience. Since I completely changed the configuration of desks, and therefore the sightlines of my students, I did what most teachers never do in their own classrooms: I sat in every desk in the room.

The benefits of this exercise were astounding. I was able to gauge, immediately, whether a student sitting in each seat could hear me, see the board, see over or around someone else sitting in front or beside him or her, and see what obstacles—physical or otherwise—might hamper his or her learning experience in my classroom. I experienced the overall perspective on the entire environment I was creating in the classroom; and I could make adjustments where necessary. Not only did I get an instant education in regard to their sightlines, I gained immediate and unforgettable insight into what it meant to occupy a seat as a student in my very own class.

This experience taught me much about my environment.

Walls

What teachers choose to place on the walls of their classrooms, believe it or not, makes a tremendous difference in students' lives. In a perfect world, students would be rapt with attention to every lesson and hang on every teacher's word. This simply is not reality. When students' attention begins to wane, and their vision begins to wander around the room, the wise teacher has something interesting, educational, and/or inspirational on the walls for the students to peruse, consider, or reflect on.

I have a personal example of how crucial this can be. I had a wonderful eleventh grade English teacher, Mrs. Geba, who taught us American literature. Even in this interesting class with a motivating teacher, my focus was known to wander from time to time. When this intellectual lethargy overcame me, I would check out other things in the room. What I noticed, mostly, was that I wasn't the only one who had strayed. Maybe Lorna was brushing her hair. Maybe Greg was talking to Jon. Maybe Trish was computing her softball stats. When all else failed, I scanned any flat surface for reading material.

My teacher had a small poster on her podium. It was one of those typical, educational-style posters (usually made by a company called Argus) that had the greeting card scene of a beautiful orange and red sunset with a quaint saying in script letters. Most teachers had posters like this on their walls, and we read them once if at all and never noticed them again. This time, though, the message stuck with me. The poster said simply, "Happiness is a means of traveling, not a destination."

It was an epiphany.

Previously, I had been saying to myself, "When this or that happens, then I will be happy" or "When I get this or that, then I will be happy," and so forth. When I finally gave the saying on that poster some thought (remember, it had probably been there for the entire year and I only just then stopped to actually ponder it), what it had to say spoke to me and changed my whole approach to life. I realized that I needed to make happiness an aspect of the way I journeyed through life and not just expect that certain material possessions or fulfilled goals would bring an ultimate (and ultimately, unfulfilling) kind of happiness. I had to find happiness in the small things of everyday life and incorporate them into my approach to the trip I was making through the world. I remember a lot from Mrs. Geba's English class, but what I learned from that simple wall decoration was invaluable.

That poster has made me a happier person for over twenty years now.

Did Mrs. Geba expect her little podium poster to have such a profound and long-lasting effect on one of her students? I don't know. Was anyone else affected the way I was by that poster or any others in the school? I don't know that, either. What I do know is that because Mrs. Geba consciously attempted to create a physical environment where it might be easier for her students to learn, one of them learned something which permanently—and positively—changed his perspective on life for his entire existence.

Not bad for one day in American lit.

The logistical truth of the matter is that it simply takes time to amass things—like posters—to put on classroom walls. The first two years of my teaching career my walls remained embarrassingly, and antiseptically, white. I felt like I was teaching in an operating room. As a beginning teacher, I had few posters and virtually no money to buy anything but the most necessary of educational supplies.

A few years went by, though, and then not only could I afford a few colorful posters (that of course I hoped would have the same effect on my students that Mrs. Geba's poster had on me), but by then, I learned another valuable lesson about making the most of my classroom environment: Student projects make great posters.

Student projects yield a number of highly attractive and colorful pieces of work which can be displayed on counters and walls that will not only dress them up physically, but will please your students and provide them with an improved sense of self-esteem when they see the pride with which you display their creative efforts. I have done comic strips for *Animal Farm*, collages for *The Catcher in the Rye*, character posters for our mythology unit, and masks for *Lord of the Flies*.

Since discovering the benefits of displaying my students' work, and the improvement it makes in the physical environment of my classroom, my walls have rarely been blank since.

I'd like to think Mrs. Geba would be proud of me.

23

READING ALOUD

Most of us enjoyed being read to when we were young. Maybe we sat enthralled as our parents or some other adult figure in our lives read to us from a storybook before bed. Or it could have been as simple as being read to by a "Mr. Rogers" type star of a children's show. One of the joys of my life is reading to my two daughters. I'm the one who sulks away, disappointed, when they want to stop.

The misconception is that when we grow up, we no longer enjoy the experience of being read to. We view it as somehow too childish or beneath us to be read to by someone else.

Educational research says that my generation has largely strayed from the habit of reading to the children in *our* lives. The impact of this was made clear when a colleague related the following story: To teach the literary device of parody, this teacher instructed her students to write a parody of a nursery rhyme. While everyone seemed to understand the concept of parody, very few of her students could remember being read to as children at all, let alone come up with a nursery rhyme they could use as a model to spoof.

Reading aloud to one's students may also seem like the sacred domain of the English teacher, but teachers from many other subject areas can help their students learn by using the performance technique of reading to their students. Reading aloud need not be restricted strictly to literature. Teachers can read from textbooks, articles or criticism, or even current events as reported in magazines or newspapers. This chapter will suggest a few helpful hints that will ensure that, if you choose to read aloud, the message will be communicated successfully. Because reading aloud is basically a total performance in itself, these will sound like mini-versions of other techniques mentioned in this book.

Book Placement

Hold the book at chest level and cast your eyes down at the page when you need to read the next section. Positioning the book this way increases the chances your voice will carry over the book and that you will be heard. The mistake many people make when reading aloud is holding the book as if they were reading it to themselves—namely, directly in front of their own face. This causes their voice to be sent straight into the book where the pages absorb all sound, instead of it being projected out into the audience where it belongs. When reading aloud, then, make certain you are speaking *over* the book and not *into* it.

Secondly, while reading aloud it is a good idea to use appropriate facial expressions to further communicate whatever story is being told. Holding the book at chest level allows the audience to see your face, thereby giving them a deeper understanding of the key ideas and feelings in the story as well as a more thorough enjoyment of your performance of it.

Establish Eye Contact

Eye contact plays a fundamental part in reading aloud successfully. While your voice, and what you choose to do with it, is one method of bonding with your audience when reading aloud, eye contact with the audience can make the difference as to whether or not you communicate your message to the audience at all. As you read, memorize brief phrases and short sentences, so that you may look up and around at those you're reading to. Use your facial and vocal expressions to emphasize the message and the tone of what you're reading. In this case, the audience is receiving the message through three channels: textually (the written word), verbally (vocal inflection and expression), and visually (through eye contact). They are, therefore, more likely to retain the information.

Maintaining periodic eye contact with your audience sends a message which says, "I'm still aware you're out there listening, and I want to connect with you." Another message it sends is, "I'm checking to see if you're still with me because what I'm telling you is important." We do the same thing when we talk to someone. We establish eye contact to make a connection and to check if our partner is listening and comprehending what we're saying.

While establishing and maintaining eye contact with the audience is a polite part of performance etiquette when reading aloud, it is possible to overdo it. Watch the television news sometime. The anchorpeople have TelePrompters from which they read when they do the news. A little television screen is positioned directly in the eye of the camera. The anchorperson can see the TelePrompter, but the home audience cannot. There is no reason that the anchorperson would ever have to look down at his or her copy because it is all written on the screen directly in front of him or her. Yet newscasters do periodically look down at the copy they hold in their hands because it's what people are used to seeing, and it makes the newscaster seem more human. The people at home would be more than a little disturbed if they thought the anchorpeople had the news completely memorized! This is just another method to ensure that the audience is being given the information in the most palatable format possible.

When you establish eye contact in the classroom, avoid the shotgun approach. Don't merely look up and take in the class as a single unit. Choose individuals and focus on their eyes during the times you look up from the text. Choose different sides of the room—left and right, front and back—each time you look up. Varying the way in which you establish eye contact will improve your performance and give your reading depth, meaning, and soul.

Use the Space

There are two steps a reader can take physically to ensure a successful reading: move around and stay still. While these steps may seem paradoxical, they both can improve a reading, depending on when and where they are practiced. For example, if the tone of the piece is loud, energetic, and frenetic, the reader can mirror this tone by making sure to move around the room to keep readers intrigued and keep their minds moving as swiftly as the story is. This approach is good for actions scenes, chases, debates, arguments—anywhere the tension and/ or energy builds to a peak.

Conversely, if there is a quiet, dramatic, or serious moment that deserves a serious reading or where the author is attempting to establish a certain mood, absolute stillness can be very effective for creating a powerful moment in the piece. Absolute stillness rivets an audience's attention to what is being said and forces them to contemplate its meaning. I stand still when I know that what I'm reading is key information in a story or novel and I want to be certain my students are listening to it. I move around, on the other hand, when I want energy, excitement, and passion.

The stillness approach is good for most any climax in any chapter, poem, story, or novel. It is equally useful, however, for scenes involving deaths, confessions, romantic moments, or good-byes. When I read the scene where George shoots Lennie in *Of Mice and Men*, I barely twitch an eyelash. I want to remove myself from my students' experience of this moment. I want my students to be moved by the tragic, and ultimately generous, moment Steinbeck invokes in the ending of his novel.

Explore Relationships

There are two distinct ways of exploring relationships in a reading: physically and verbally.

Identify relationships in a reading *physically* by standing in one place for one character (or in the case of an article, one side of a debate, argument, etc.) and standing in another place for another character or argument or position. Also, you can stand in one area to indicate where a character in a novel is and move to another area to indicate some kind of change in that character's life (indicating that he or she is, at least figuratively, in "another place").

The second way to illustrate relationships is *verbally*. Use one character voice (see chapter 15) for one character and other voices for a second, third, or fourth character. In the case of an article or textbook, use one tone, attitude, pitch, or volume for one position, point, or argument, and a second one for any other positions or points made. When establishing relationships while reading a piece of literature, always consider the following: What type of relationship do the characters have (father/son, boss/employee, priest/confessor)? Who has the power? What are the emotions of the piece you're reading? The answers to these questions will effectively color your reading choices and make your reading a greater success.

Perfect Your Projection

Make sure they can hear you. If they can't, you're wasting your time.

Pause for Effect

Knowing when to pause for effect can impact your reading and increase your audience's understanding. Many times we've heard people reading too quickly and as if all of the information had the same value. They did not emphasize important points or de-emphasize unimportant points. They just read along as if everything counted exactly as much as what came before. Their reading had the same effect on the audience as a drive through the Arizona desert—everything looked exactly the same until the sameness become mind-numbingly boring.

You can avoid this trap by learning when to pause for effect. The most important information is usually at the end of a sentence or paragraph; therefore, it is critical that you emphasize these words and read the last few words in a sentence with energy and volume and then stop to let the information "sink in" to the audience before proceeding.

Check this theory for accuracy by pulling any book off the shelf and opening to any page and reading a sentence out loud at random. Now read it a second time. Only this time, identify the most important information in the sentence. Not only will you find that the last part of the sentence probably contains the most important information, but you will discover that if you pause just before saying the last part (or just after)—as well as "punching" that information with volume, energy, and expression when you *do* say it—you will have provided that sentence with more power and zip than if you read all of the words with the same value.

Reading aloud in the classroom can be an enriching experience for both teacher and student. By smoothly combining the methods mentioned above into a cohesive reading style, you can enhance not only your classroom performance technique but, with any luck, your students' love of the written word.

24

ROLE-PLAYING

We all perform roles. Everyday of our lives we are performing the roles of son, daughter, boyfriend, girlfriend, boss, employee, or any of a hundred of other roles that not only help define who we are but help us know how to behave. In short, our roles provide us with a rule book; they tell us what and what not to do in any given situation.

Knowing how to play certain roles keeps us from acting inappropriately. In the role of minister, for instance, we would know to be serious, respectful, and approach situations from a spiritual perspective. We would know never to laugh during the eulogy for the dearly departed. In the role of employee, we should be punctual, hardworking, and motivated. We should never make and distribute photocopies of our co-workers' W-2 forms. And in the role of boyfriend, of course, we should be kind, caring, and loving. It would be a mistake, on the other hand, to go on and on in front of our significant other about what a succulent mouth Cyndi Crawford has.

Sometimes it is beneficial to play roles we don't normally play, in order to see things from another perspective. In *To Kill a Mockingbird*, Atticus Finch tells his children they can never truly understand a person until they, "walked around in that person's shoes."

Actors are in the business of taking on roles. In one film or stage play, an actor may play a romantic leading man, while in another he may play an assassin for a communist country (Of course in some films, that's the same character!). Actors walk around in other people's shoes for a living.

In the classroom, role-playing refers to when students improvise a short scene or, in some cases, write a short piece, while adopting the persona or role of someone else. They can take on the role of a character in a book, a celebrity or public figure, or—in some cases—teacher of the class. One of the most immediate benefits of using role-playing in the classroom is that students are able to gain a new perspective on the material by allowing themselves to look at it through someone else's eyes. They see what others see, and this usually gives them new and different insights into the instructional material.

On the surface, then, the concept of role-playing may not seem like a performance technique for teachers. Usually, teaches assign their students roles and have them act out improvised scenes. The teacher's role is usually supervisory and non-participatory.

Role-playing is actually the most obvious opportunity for the teacher to do some real acting. The easiest way for a teacher to include role-playing in a lesson plan is to come into class and, using appropriate costumes and props, adopt the persona of a person, character, or figure relevant to the material she is teaching and to give a section of a lecture as that character. This works for all subject areas. Certainly, as an English teacher, I could be Jay Gatsby, Romeo, King Midas, or Hamlet. Math and science teachers can throw on a lab coat and glasses and be Einstein, J. Robert Oppenheimer, or Carl Sagan. They can throw on a toga and be Hippocrates or Pythagoras.

One teacher on our campus plays George Washington each year, as well as a number of other historical characters who figure prominently in the period of history he covers. He uses hats, coats, shoes, boots, and other costume parts, as well as small, easy-to-find props such as glasses, canes, and swords to make the subject matter come alive for his students. Once, I even saw him leaving the teacher's lounge dressed as the Statue of Liberty, complete with concrete gray crown, torch, and tablet. During this unit he also makes over his entire classroom to resemble Ellis Island.

I include role-playing as a viable performance technique for teachers, therefore, because role-playing can increase the dramatic intensity of a teacher's course content and improve the overall "stage presence" of that teacher's instructional style. It can also be considered a valid performance technique for teachers if, in fact, teachers actually participate in it with their students. Unfortunately, teachers are usually more concerned with maintaining that professional "distance" as teacher and do not deign to do what they are asking their students to do, for fear of looking both foolish or losing that sense of business-like dignity they so value. While this is certainly a legitimate position in many cases, sometimes teachers use it as a crutch to hide their performance anxiety.

I use role-playing in my class frequently throughout the year. As a teacher of literature, there are a number of times I have my students write from the persona of a character in the book we're studying. For example, while reading *The Scarlet Letter,* I have them write a letter from Arthur Dimmesdale to Hester Prynne justifying his behavior. Also during my unit on The Puritans, I perform "Sinners in the Hands of Angry God," as if I were Puritan preacher Jonathan Edwards. I stand behind my podium and deliver the sermon as a fire-and-brimstone evangelist. I yell, cajole, and gesticulate my way through about four or five paragraphs to give them an idea of what it was like to sit in a Puritan congregation on a Sunday morning.

During oral presentations, I may have students take on the "role" of teacher and present material to the class. My juniors usually have a relatively easy time identifying with Holden Caulfield in *The Catcher in the Rye,* so at the end of our unit, I have the students take on the roles of the characters in the book and act out scenes—Holden with Mr. Spencer, his teacher; Holden and Horowitz, the caustic cabdriver; Holden and Phoebe, his sister, etc. Not only are these short skits a lot of fun for the students, but they come away with a deeper understanding and memory of the scenes in the book and of Holden's mental and emotional state at the time. When the mood strikes me, I also jump in and take a role during these skits—I have fun and kids love to see me participating.

Many other subjects lend themselves well to role-playing. Our career and family studies teacher, for example, has mentioned using skits and role-playing to practice assertiveness skills. Other social studies teachers use role-playing for mock trials, historical events, and job interview practice.

The mock job interview is particularly effective. One student—or maybe the teacher—plays the boss, while another student is the employee candidate. They spend ten minutes or so improvising a job interview. This allows students to practice interview skills in a safe and non-judgmental atmosphere. This way they can make all of the errors they need to make during a practice session and not during an interview where an actual job is on the line.

A history teacher I know also uses diary-style entries to have her students write from the perspective of an historical character ("You are living in 1774. Write a colonial diary of your experiences."). Our German teacher uses role-playing at the end of every unit, so students can practice their German in a conversational setting.

We play roles every day of our lives. Take a risk. Play a role other than "teacher" in your classroom.

25

MOOD

1. *The houselights are on, the orchestra is tuning up in the orchestra pit, the crowd is humming with chatter and coughs, and the air is electric with the flipping of program pages. A few last stragglers step down the aisles on the way to their seats…Suddenly the houselights dim, the orchestra quiets, a hush falls over the theater as the crowd grows still and silent in anticipation, the coughing and murmuring stop instantly, the programs are stilled in the audience's laps, and all heads turn toward the stage in unison. There is a beat, then the curtain rises.*

2. *The stadium is full to capacity, the lights illuminating the stands are so bright it feels like midday, the announcer introduces the vocalist, everyone rises and listens or sings along to the National Anthem, the umpire yells, "Play ball!" The crowd cheers. Later, the P.A. system plays a thundering version of dun dun dun da da dun da dun da da dun da…and, in unison, the crowd yells, "CHARGE!"*

3. *The pounding backbeat rocking the darkened arena seems like it's been going for hours. The crowd is wild with anticipation and is cheering wildly for the main event. Just when it seems like the audience has reached its peak and will explode with expectation, the show lights erupt on the stage, the band is silhouetted in a blinding white light, and just after a disembodied voice yells out the name of the band, the members of the group are lit on stage like candles on a cake and the lead singer screams, "Hello, Cleveland! Are you reading to rock?!?!?" As*

the crowd lifts the roof off the arena, the band launches into the first song.

These three scenarios illustrate how important setting the mood is for guaranteeing the success of any performance. Whether sports, music, acting, or even teaching, creating anticipation in the audience ensures that your performance will enjoy focused and attentive viewers and listeners. In each of the situations above, light, sound, or physical conditions have been put in place to create anticipation, excitement, almost a yearning or desire for the event to begin. There is no reason why we can't use similar theatrical conventions in the classroom and create that same kind of excitement for our students.

There are two aspects to establishing mood in the classroom. The first concerns the physical structure (classroom) and the materials we use. Without realizing it, we manipulate our classroom environment every day to aid our lessons, so why not take a more cognizant approach with the elements we have at our disposal? Teachers can take advantage of such elements as lighting, music, props, costumes, volume—both loud and soft (to set a mood, lowering your voice is as critical as raising it)—and yes, even silence. Using silence to establish mood, especially at the beginning of an activity or class, is very effective and very inexpensive!

The second aspect to setting mood concerns the teacher's personal emotions. You can control the mood set for each day, lesson, or unit by recognizing and understanding your own disposition. If you're mood is good, there's a better chance your students' moods will be good, too. If you're cranky, tired, or depressed, however, that mood can't help but infiltrate the rest of the class. Be wary of the mood you're projecting and make certain it's the one you intend.

If we think back, not only to the most memorable performances we've attended in our life but to the most memorable classes we've witnessed, we'll see how large a role the mood played in our appreciation. Not only did the established mood help us enjoy these classes or lessons at the time, but it helped create an indelible image we carry with us today.

Case in point: It was the end of October during seventh grade. Halloween was right around the corner. Mr. Itson took the entire seventh grade into our windowless music room (I attended a very small junior high school). From the time he picked us up, he was very somber and quiet; his persona, almost eerily still. When we were all inside the music room, we were arranged in a circle around Mr. Itson. Suddenly, the lights went out. It was so dark, I remember, I couldn't see my hand in front of my face. From out of the darkness, there suddenly came a small light. Mr. Itson had lit a candle and was holding it in his lap. His face twisted in weird and distorted shapes. His eyes leapt and danced creepily in the candlelight. Slowly, methodically, weirdly, Mr. Itson began to speak: "True!—Nervous—very, very dreadfully nervous as I had been and am!"

From memory, he recited Edgar Allan Poe's, "The Tell-Tale Heart."

It was an incredibly dramatic and theatrical performance. At times he would boom out the lines and we would shudder with the volume and vibration of his voice. Other times he would use a stage whisper, lowering his volume and drawing us in so that we had to lean closer to hear. Mr. Itson, who I knew as a teacher and not as a performer or lover of literature, took the time to set the mood of the performance—from the moment he picked us up to the moment he finished the story. Because of his attention to mood, I've never forgotten his performance and have liked that story ever since—over two decades ago!

A teacher friend of mine tells of a colleague who set the mood for his eighth grade English class with a moment of silence everyday before they began the day's activities. When his students came in from outside, he required them to sit still in their desks and be absolutely silent for sixty seconds. After that single minute of silence, the teacher claimed the students were more focused, calm, and worked more quietly overall than on those occasions when they didn't observe that small ritual.

Create a mood. Do not allow the state of mind or feeling or the predominant spirit in your classroom be random or accidental. Choose the mood you wish your students to experience. Introduce that mood and share it with your students to enliven and enrich your message.

If you are still skeptical about the role mood plays in making a classroom performance memorable, think back to your favorite classes or teachers. Try to recapture that feeling you experienced at the beginning of every class period: the anticipation, the thrill of wondering where the class was going to go that day, the yearning for things to get started. Those teachers knew about establishing mood. Furthermore, you remember what you learned in those classes, in part, because of the mood set by the teacher. Allow your students to have the same experience in your classroom.

26

HUMOR

The ability to laugh is a gift from the gods and the ability to appreciate humor is a blessing. Laughter can be a shield against pain in this life and a weapon against difficult times. It can make a bad situation tolerable and a good situation, unforgettable.

Humor is all around us. The key is to recognize and acknowledge it.

Life is so much funnier than anything that ever came out of a writer's head. Life has ready-made jokes for the taking and laughter is around every corner—literally. One day I was driving to the store and turned my head in time to look down a side street. A man stood over the open hood of his car while a white plume of smoke undulated toward the heavens. At that split second, he threw his arms up in an exaggerated show of frustration and helplessness. I related to his exasperation with an uncooperative and unpredictable vehicle and, therefore, my recognition of his extreme situation made his gesture very funny.

Once I was in Las Vegas with my wife and in-laws. As we drove along, we noticed a motorcycle cop in full regalia—black and gold helmet, knee-high boots, mirrored sunglasses—pulling a motorist over. Just as the cop dismounted from his motorcycle and approached the driver's side of the vehicle, the theme from "Dragnet" started playing on our car radio. We immediately burst into laughter. The irony of the serious, law-and-order music and the authoritative attitude and attire of the traffic cop made this scene hilarious.

The natural spontaneity and reality of these true life situations is funnier than anything that could have ever been put down on paper.

Humor can—and should—be found in the classroom as well. Humor can be a positive addition to any lesson plan and almost any topic. In fact, my fondest memories of former teachers are of those who used humor as an effective tool in their teaching style.

My high school Spanish teacher, for example, is still my favorite teacher of all time. Mr. Morrissey was knowledgeable, compassionate, and a good communicator (in two languages, no less!). Aside from those qualities, he was also one of the funniest teachers I've every known. Later, when I became a substitute teacher and taught Spanish classes myself, I found myself imitating Mr. Morrissey's timing, delivery, and mannerisms.

During the first week of Introduction to Spanish, Mr. Morrissey had us do some choral response work, just to acquaint us with the sound and rhythm of the new language. He'd say something in Spanish, we would repeat it, and then he'd translate it into English.

That week the following exchange took place:

Mr. Morrissey: Como estas?
Class: Como estas?
Mr. Morrissey: How are you? (pause) Estoy bien.
Class: Estoy bien.
Mr. Morrissey: I am fine. (pause) Senor Morrissey es el rey.
Class: Senor Morrissey is el rey.
Mr. Morrissey (*straight-faced*): Mr. Morrissey is the king.
(class erupts in laughter)

As in the construction of any classic joke, Mr. Morrissey took us down the road we were expecting to travel and then—at the right moment—he made a sharp turn which threw us off course, resulting in the humor of the situation.

Is humor a good teaching technique? That exchange took place twenty two years ago, and I still remember both the joke and the Spanish he was trying to teach us. Mr. Morrissey taught us that not only could we have fun learning Spanish, but that we could just have fun *learning*.

Humor is such an effective tool, in fact, that I use it in my own classroom every chance I get. Recently, for example, I was teaching J.D. Salinger's *The Catcher in the Rye* to my juniors. In the novel, there are three teenage boys: Holden Caulfield, the protagonist; Ward Stradlater, his dorm roommate; and Robert Ackley, the geeky kid from down the hall.

I wrote all three names on the board and drew columns between them. Next, we brainstormed words or characteristics that might describe each character—Holden (sarcastic, failure, lonely, sensitive, etc.), Stradlater (vain, jock, conceited, self-centered, etc.), and Ackley (annoying, gross, whining, etc.).

Attempting to make a connection between the book and their lives, I explained that while—at times—we might all feel like Holden, we might also know a stuck-up, vain, jock-type like Stradlater or a nerdy, annoying dork like Ackley.

"Did you know people like that in high school?" asked a student in the back row.

"Certainly," I said.

"Who were *you* most like?" another student asked.

"Well," I began, pointing toward Stradlater's name on the board. "I certainly knew people like Stradlater. People who were athletic, well-built, popular, and good-looking." Then, as I spoke the next line, I moved my hand over toward Ackley's name on the board, an early physical indication that I was more like him. "But I was really more like...(then, dropping my hand to my side)...Holden, actually. I always felt a lot like Holden." I lead the class to expect their teacher had been a geeky, awkward adolescent and then, by misdirecting them, caused them to laugh—and hopefully remember a smidgen on what we were discussing.

According to *Theater: A Contemporary Approach* by Jerry V. Pickering, there are at least five different ways to create surefire moments of comedy—incongruity, surprise, exaggeration, repetition, and wisecrack. While wisecracks and surprise can be used effectively by the correct practitioner, using these techniques can be a risky maneuver. Several of my high school teachers used wisecracks and surprise to get laughs, but usually it was to insult a student (wisecracks) or make someone the unwitting butt of a joke (surprise). In both cases, they managed to undermine student confidence and self-esteem.

Teachers will also probably not create much humor through the use of repetition because they realize that—save for rare cases—it is too easy for young students to confuse a teacher's using repetition for impact and effect with "a really boring lesson." ("That Mr. Tricarico's a really nice guy and all, but he keeps repeating himself!"). Not to mention that repetition—in the wrong hands—can be disastrous.

Incongruity and exaggeration, however, can be used effectively to elicit humor in a classroom environment and will usually enhance an atmosphere of learning and understanding.

<u>Incongruity</u>

Incongruity occurs whenever there is a departure from the expected. Most of the jokes office workers tell around the water cooler rely on incongruity and misdirection. Most classic stand-up comedy bits rely on a departure from the expected:

The doctor told me I was going to die. I told him I wanted a second opinion. He said, "Fine. You're ugly, too."

This guy came up to me on the street and told me he hadn't had a bite in three days…so I bit him."

In both of these examples, the audience is given information which leads them to a certain expectation; a certain norm. The listener is set up to believe that the payoff will be an appropriate one. Then, at the last possible moment, the storyteller throws the listener a curve which is *incongruous* with the expectation.

Using incongruity in class can set up or clarify teaching points or concepts in an unexpected and humorous way. As illustrated in *The Catcher in the Rye* example above, incongruity can lead students to question assumptions, dissemble stereotypes, and rethink certain paradigms. Most methods of comedy rely, to some degree, on the element of incongruity to generate humor.

Exaggeration

There are certain elements of life everyone recognizes and accepts as our collective reality. Exaggeration relies on amplifying those recognizable elements to drastic and absurd proportions. This division between the norm and the exaggeration—this *incongruity*, if you will—contradicts our expectations and is, therefore, funny. Exaggeration, then, is the embellishment of reality to a ridiculous degree. Much like incongruity, exaggeration is a deviation from our collective expectations.

Exaggeration is a fun technique for teachers to use to elicit humor in their classrooms. For example, the 11th grade teachers in our English department are expected to show a four part filmed version of *The Scarlet Letter* by Nathaniel Hawthorne. While the movie is well-done, the pace is pretty dreadful. I know my students recognize this (remember, we're talking about a generation raised on the 15-second sound bite on the news and television commercials that rely on rapid-fire, MTV-influenced editing). If after Part I was over I said, "Hang in there, class—only three sections," I would be telling the truth and they would certainly know what they were in for. Usually, though, I want them to know I understand how awful the pace is, so I'll say something like, "Well, class, only 37 parts to go..."

This exaggeration is beneficial for a number of reasons. First of all, if they know that I'll occasionally make a joke, they might start to feel that the class is fun and that it might actually be worth listening to the old man up front. Secondly, they will realize teachers do not consider *all* educational materials sacrosanct and above criticism. Thirdly, they might start to have faith in the "We're all in this together" feeling I try so hard to create. A little humor can go a long way toward developing a collective sense of purpose and a feeling of community.

The Rule of Threes

The Rule of Threes is another classic comedy structure that teachers can use in the classroom to make their students enjoy learning through laughter. Even people unfamiliar with comedy will probably recognize The Rule of Threes. How many times have you been sitting in the faculty lounge and Bob, the really annoying guy from science (or English or math), comes up and says, "I gotta a good one for ya," and then launches into some off-color joke which usually begins, "A priest, a rabbi, and a minister…" or "An Italian, an American, and a whatever (choose the ethnic group of your choice—whoever's being mocked this decade.) Most anecdotal jokes you've ever heard repeat a situation twice in the set-up and then deviate from the norm in the third situation, which results in the punch line.

As an example:

Bob, Sheila, and Joe are stranded in the desert. They find an old bottle, rub it, and out pops a genie.

"I've been in that bottle for 2,000 years," the genie says, "For releasing me, I will grant you each one wish."

They all agree that they want to get out of the desert, but the genie says he can't do that.

"In that case," says Bob, "I would like an unlimited supply of water, so whenever it gets hot I can drink to quench my thirst. (1)

"And I," says Sheila, "would like a fan that runs by itself, so when it gets hot, I can always have cool air to blow in my face." (2)

"And I," says Joe, "would like a car door."
Everyone looks at him.
"That way," Joe says, "whenever it gets hot, I can roll down the window." (3)

The Rule of Threes is as old as comedy itself: Larry, Moe, and Curly; Huey, Dewey, and Louie; and, of course, Reagan, Bush, and Clinton. (Notice how stunningly I worked both incongruity and The Rule of Threes into that last example!).

The classroom is the perfect place for The Rule of Threes. Teachers are always dealing with lists of things: books, assignments, roll sheets, etc. Teachers can make students laugh by insuring that the third element in a list in incongruous to the two which set it up.

An example:

This semester class, we will be reading three books: Animal Farm *by George Orwell,* The Great Gatsby *by F. Scott Fitzgerald, and finally, the shortest book of the year,* My Favorite Liberals *by G. Gordon Liddy.*

Two set-ups to establish the norm, deviation on the third situation for the pay-off.

The Rule of Threes.

Humor also has very therapeutic effects in the classroom. An amusing or lighthearted comment by the teacher can help make tough concepts more manageable. The right joke at the right time can relieve mounting pressure—for both teacher and students—when a lesson is not working as planned.

Humor can also diffuse anger. If tempers flare, a properly placed exaggeration or incongruity can lighten up the mood almost immediately. One of my favorite examples is when two students exchange words in the classroom and look as if they might start fighting (usually boys, but not always). When I first notice them arguing, I'll observe them for a moment or two and give them a chance to work it out without my intervention. If they settle it, I'll go back to what I was doing without comment (or, maybe, with a discreet and sincere question: "Everything okay over there?"). If they start to push and shove, however, I call them both by name—loudly and firmly: "Justin and Nick!" They usually turn and look, red-faced from the scuffle, steam still billowing out of their ears. I look them in the eye and say sternly: "You know my rules: no dancing in the classroom!" This is usually silly enough to cause them to laugh and breaks the tempest of violence that was brewing.

The effective use of humor in the classroom will help the teacher create a fun, pleasant and enjoyable atmosphere in which students can learn. Humor helps us deal better with the stressors of the educational process, eases the pressures of teaching and learning, and reduces the anger and hostilities everyone faces in the classroom.

While it is certainly not our job as teachers to spend five hours a day simply entertaining our students, it is equally true that no one ever said that education *couldn't* be fun. A teacher with a sense of humor can be a mentor who stays with us long past high school.

Just ask Mr. Morrissey.

27

CONCENTRATION AND LISTENING

The perennial hope of the teacher is that students are concentrating and listening. What we often fail to realize, however, is how these same two behaviors, when *we* perform them, not only improve our performance styles, but our overall teaching process. In addition, when we perform these two behaviors outside of the classroom, we improve our personal lives, as well.

Concentration

When Robert DeNiro, Al Pacino, or Meryl Streep give such fine performances, at the heart lies the power of concentration. Concentration gives performances their energy, intensity, and value. Concentration makes the content of performances matter. The excellent focus of these actors and their fine concentration on details of characterization make their performances brilliant. Solid concentration is one of the performance elements that really sets these actors apart.

Everything else, of course, must be in place for this to work. Lines and blocking must be learned, character and script analysis must be explored, and performance choices must be finely honed during the rehearsal process.

Preparation plus concentration equals an optimum performance.

The dictionary defines the verb "concentrate" as, "to employ all of one's thoughts or attention or effort on something." I like this definition for a number of reasons. First of all, I love that the word "concentrate" is a verb. I believe it is an action. To concentrate is to do; to take steps to make sure one is choosing to direct all of one's attention to a single activity, ideas, or person. Secondly, I like how all-encompassing this definition sounds. To concentrate, then, is to employ all of one's thought or attention or effort. Not some, not a pretty big amount, not even most.

All.

When skilled actors concentrate they focus all they have on the given moment. That's why intense concentration makes good acting.

A teacher with excellent concentration skills will also give a good performance in the classroom. If a teacher's entire thoughts, attention, and effort are focused on the topic, not only will students be more engaged and less distracted, they will also retain more information than if the teacher's attention is diffused, cloudy, or unfocused.

If you have ever watched a cat focus on a piece of fluff drifting through the air, you have seen the paramount example of concentration. Everything in that cat's attention is subordinated to that piece of fluff. Nothing else enters the cat's perception. As spectators of said feline, our attention is also invariably drawn to whatever the cat is watching so intensely and riveted to it.

In other words, good concentration is contagious.

If teachers are intensely focused on the material, there is a better chance they will be able to focus their students' attention as well. Students do not like to be left behind intellectually, whatever they may say or however they may behave. They want to be riveted to what the cat is watching (and hopefully, what the teacher is offering is more than a piece of fluff drifting through the air).

Good concentration is also synergistic. If teacher and students are focused in a unified way on a single activity or idea, whatever the end product or result, it will be larger, better, greater, and more valuable than if only the teacher or only the student were concentrating on it. Where concentration is concerned, two heads are truly better than one.

Try this: Sit in a quiet room and close your eyes. Access the breath impulse and find your breathing rhythm. Clear your mind and thoughts. Next, using just your listening skills, listen to whatever sounds you are hearing. All of your concentration should be focused on those sounds. Finally, attempt to identify the source of those sounds and how far away the sound might be coming from (the buzz of an airplane overhead, the whirr of a vacuum cleaner from the condo upstairs, the rush of the traffic on the Interstate a mile away, etc.). After practice, you will find that your concentration and listening skills have heightened and that by occasionally using this technique you will increase your ability to focus "all your thoughts or attention or effort," thereby improving your stage presence in the classroom. Students will be riveted to your energy and mesmerized by your message.

Listening

For an actor to give a realistic and believable performance, he or she must listen—not just hear, but really *listen*—to his or her partner in any given scene. Even if the actor has heard each line a million times, each night he must listen to the nuance, meaning, and inflection (to say nothing of the body language and attitude) of his partner onstage as if it were the very first time the words were uttered. It is the immediacy and urgency of the moment which makes the performance believable. Actors must listen to each other onstage to insure the purity and the reality of their reactions.

Listening is an equally important quality for a classroom teacher to possess. Teachers can spend an inordinate amount of time talking *at* their students, via lectures, instructions, guided practice, etc. But these same teachers, while quite gifted, can be woefully negligent in truly *listening* to what those students are saying in return.

Listening to the student involves more than just hearing the words. Good listening involves:

- *Empathy*. You must put yourself in the place of the other person and really try to comprehend what that person is saying, what he or she is going through, and how he or she is being affected.

- *Eye contact*. Eye contact shows you care enough about what the person is saying to focus all your attention on what he or she is saying.

- *Questioning*. Ask questions for clarification of ideas or concepts you do not understand. This shows your willingness to understand and creates trust in the other person.

- *Paraphrasing*. One of the best methods to make it clear you understand the message is to put it into your own words. If you paraphrase the message you've received ("What I hear you saying, then, is…"), the other person can correct or clarify any concept which was not communicated effectively.

When used correctly these aspects of listening will improve the quality of your communication with your students, guaranteeing that a higher percentage of the material you teach them will be received and understood.

Many of the behavior or achievement problems teachers face with their "trouble" students could be avoided or completely eliminated if the teacher practiced good listening skills. Good listening skills on the part of the teacher create a valuable form of trust between the student and the teacher, which never fails to pay dividends down the line.

To further understand good listening skills, however, it is critical to understand the communication process.

Communication is a circular process. Just because you say something to someone, you cannot assume that communication has taken place. That's only the first step in the process. For communication to be successful, the message you send out must be processed by the receiver, acknowledged, and then returned.

There are four parts to effective communication:

1. A sends a message to B

2. B acknowledges (through questioning or paraphrasing) that the message has been received

3. B sends a new message back to A (which usually involves feedback on the original message)

4. A acknowledges that the message has been received (A sends feedback, B acknowledges, etc.)

It is this circular pattern of message/acknowledgement/feedback/ new message that makes for successful communication. However, when a teacher sends a message and just assumes it has been received without requesting feedback, he or she is ignoring *three-quarters* of the process.

Similarly, when a student begins to tell the teacher why an assignment has not come in or why it was necessary to be late or why a book is overdue, the teacher will "turn off" in many cases, assuming he or she has "heard it all before." This approach denies the individual circumstance that may make a difference.

Even if the excuse is of the "my-dog-ate-my-homework" variety, good listening skills will help the teacher maintain a strong and positive relationship with the student that may help the student perform better in the future, knowing that he or she has a teacher who "really listens."

Once, early in my career, I was trying to help a student with a worksheet on figurative language, specifically similes. After ten or fifteen minutes of wrestling with the concepts on the worksheet, she looked up, sighed, and said, "I just don't get it, Mr. T." I felt defeated and frustrated. At length, the bell rang and I chalked it up to the one of the times I would not "reach" those within my charge and vowed that I would try harder the following day. I collected the worksheets from the desk as the class filed out the door. Just as she was leaving, however, a mischievous young boy grabbed this girl's notebook for a quick game of "keep away."

As she walked out the door, I heard her admonish him: "Steven, you give me back my notebook right now or I'm going to bust your head like a melon!"

I dropped the worksheets and raced to the door.

"That's it!" I said. "That's figurative language! You did it!"

After a few more minutes of impromptu instruction in the hallway during the passing period, I saw the light go on in her brain and, because I had been listening, we were able to succeed in teaching her the concept of similes. Ultimately, she became one of the best creative writers I've ever taught and I anticipate walking into my local bookstore one day to see her first novel sitting on the shelves.

While communication is a critical skill in teaching, there are plenty of fine teachers who are poor communicators. When teachers neglect good listening, they impair their performance the same way an actor onstage assumes what is going to be said because he or she has "heard the lines before." In both cases, the performers are shortchanging not only their partners, but themselves.

The ability to concentrate and listen are two elements of good acting, good communication, good teaching and—quite simply—good manners.

THEATRICAL
ELEMENTS

28

COSTUMES AND PROPS

Costumes and props are two of the most important aspects of performance. When actors are developing characterizations, or exploring the personalities of the persons they are portraying onstage or in film, the right costume or prop can be an enlightening addition to their work.

Aspects of character which were unclear or out of focus can, like the turning of a camera lens, come into focus as soon as the actor dresses the way the character dresses and handles what the character handles.

The crevices of the character can be illuminated with the appropriate use of both costumes and props. A hat, for instance, can unlock a door for the actor into a character's psyche and provide insight into his or her background and history. It provides a direction for an actor to follow. A person who wears a brown derby, for instance, will have a different background and behave very differently from someone who wears a backwards New York Mets baseball cap. Similarly, just the right prop—a letter opener, for example, or a fountain pen—can open a window into a character's habits, hopes, fears, and prejudices.

Similarly, when a classroom teacher uses costumes and props, they can illuminate aspects of the subject area for the student in the same manner.

Costumes

A costume is the first signal to who people are. What we wear tells people the role we will be playing for them that day. In some ways, people already wear the costumes of their professions. Doctors wear lab coats and stethoscopes; football players, a helmet, jersey, and pads; road workers, a hard hat and orange vest; the businessman, a dress shirt, slacks, necktie, and even possibly a suit or sport coat.

These costumes tell people what to expect.

There is a wonderful subplot in the movie *Teachers* where Richard Mulligan (of T.V.'s *Soap* and *Empty Nest*) plays a mental ward escapee who wanders onto a modern American high school campus and decides he is a substitute teacher for some U.S. History classes.

The joke is: no one notices the difference.

It is almost natural (and unfortunate), therefore, that during the course of the film, Mulligan's character shows much more sensitivity, creativity, and ingenuity in reaching his students than the rest of the burnt-out, jaded, and cynical veteran teachers. Much of what makes Mulligan's character so successful in the classroom is his use of performance techniques, specifically his innovative use of costumes.

In one scene, he appears as Abraham Lincoln. When the scene cuts to his class, Mulligan is wearing a full black Lincoln-esque beard and a black stovepipe hat. We come in just in time to see him applying a small, black mole to his cheek. Later, he is coming down a stairway crowded with students. He is dressed as Benjamin Franklin. He is wearing a full period costume—three-cornered hat, bifocal specs, and is carrying a huge kite with a large metal key dangling from the tail.

In one particularly hilarious scene, he is dressed as George Washington. The desks have been cleared to the side and he has placed a large canoe in the middle of the classroom. We come in as he is yelling, "Stroke! Stroke!" and his students are in the canoe with him enthusiastically stroking their leader across the Potomac River.

It is clear from their faces that the students are not only having fun, but are engaged in the learning and will not soon forget the day they rowed a canoe across their classroom.

At the end of the movie, alas, the men in white coats arrive to cart Mulligan's well-intentioned, albeit uncredentialed, substitute teacher back to the funny farm.

It's too bad, really. He was teaching them something.

As Mulligan's character illustrates, costumes can literally change the face of the average lesson plan. They can add color, depth, or humor. The effective use of a pair of glasses can make a moment in a lecture poignant, or the flamboyant use of a wig or scarf can make a tense moment more lighthearted. The use of costumes can be simple and easy or more difficult and complicated, depending on the energy, courage, and imagination of the teacher.

Our Home Economics teacher, for example, uses in her lectures an entire wardrobe of garments she's constructed in her classes. She calls them her "wearable art." I've heard of drama teachers bringing in old, white bedsheets and making everyone wear togas while they learned about Greek theater.

One of our former science teachers has 400 plus T-shirts with various images and slogans: skeletons, muscles, nerves, and quotes ("Kiss me, I don't smoke") which he slips on over his regular shirt and tie when he lectures on that particular topic. That same science teacher has graduation gowns and "lots of hats" to take on different personas which are relevant to the concepts he teaches. Similarly, an economics teacher I know uses a deerslayer (the two-sided "Sherlock Holmes" hat) to explain what he calls "economic mysteries."

The occasional use of costumes (or costume parts—a hat, a scarf, a feather boa, a pair of glasses, a leather jacket, etc.) in a classroom atmosphere can be invigorating for both teacher and student. It can liven up even the driest of lesson plans. It can wake us all up to the potential in an idea or concept and cause us to interact with the material in a fresh and novel way. Using costumes make the educational process both dramatic and entertaining for the learners in your audience.

In teaching, we get to experiment occasionally and change our costumes depending on our moods and goals for the lesson. What other profession affords this luxury? Imagine, for instance, the day we are stopped for road construction by a man holding a large red "STOP" sign who happens to be wearing a long white toga, laurel wreath, and sandals. What he is wearing would tell us that this is not the routine road construction.

Think of the message you would send if your students enter the classroom and you were wearing a motorcycle helmet and leather jacket, a parka and snow boots, or a Hawaiian shirt, pink lei, and shorts or grass skirt, while strumming a ukulele.

Wear something different in class tomorrow.

Be someone new for your students.

Props

Any physical object with which an actor must deal during the course of his performance is called a prop (short for "property"). Anything from a wallet or money to an umbrella or cane to a book or a cup of tea is considered an onstage prop. Good actors make props personal to their characters by imbuing them with emotional associations. For example, an actor might choose to believe that a cigarette case he must use in a given scene was an anniversary gift from his wife during a rocky time period in their marriage. Furthermore, he may choose to remember how the scratch in the top of the case was from when it hit the wall after his wife flung it at his head during that one fight they had the night after her birthday three years before. The actor can be as specific as she chooses. These choices will affect what she does with the prop and how she handles it. The actor will choose whatever emotional association furthers her character's motivations and objectives, just as teachers should choose props which further theirs.

In 1978, I was fifteen years old and spent one hour of my life each day in Mr. Nordell's first period Biology class. Mr. Nordell was funny (In my annual he signed, "Hope things were to your lichen. Mr. Nordell") and knowledgeable and extremely hip for a high school teacher. He had long blonde hair, a full beard and, although this is probably inaccurate because of teacher dress code expectations, I often picture him coming to class in jeans and sandals.

One day, Mr. Nordell led us into the lab room adjacent to our classroom. We passed by the sinks and microscopes and large metal tables with their tall metal stools. Finally, he gathered us around his teaching table at the front of the room. On the table sat an enormous bulbous blob of leathery-looking material. It was a creamy beige color, completely amorphous, and took up at least half of the work table. Mr. Nordell then proclaimed that what we were staring at was a healthy cow lung.

To our amazement, Mr. Nordell then took a long, clear plastic tube, inserted it into some hole in the lung that apparently only credentialed Science teachers could find, and proceeded to blow into the tube. The cow lung began to shudder on the table and then began to move as if reanimated. It began filling with air, faster than you might expect, and soon was a giant balloon of a lung sitting on top of the table. We all gaped at it dumbly until, suddenly, it sat directly at eye level.

At that time, it was one of the strangest sights I had ever seen. My fifteen year old mind half-expected Mr. Nordell to raise his arms in triumph and scream "It's alive! It's alive!"

To my disappointment, he didn't.

While Science teachers use a multitude of manipulatives every day (everything from microscopes to Bunsen burners to dissected creatures), the effective use of props can be an interesting and dramatic addition to any class in any subject matter.

A social studies teacher I know uses what she calls her "toy box" of contraceptive devices which she uses in her classes during her unit on sex education and birth control. In her Home Economics classes, she uses kitchen and sewing equipment and, of course, the best prop of all: real food.

A German teacher at our school once mentioned using real objects during new vocabulary sections. When speaking about restaurants or airports or bus stations, she tries to bring in props associated with the new vocabulary—tickets, for example, or money, or tableware.

As I mentioned, I bring in an actual conch shell for *Lord of the Flies*. This serves as an excellent visual (not to mention the auditory experience of hearing the conch when blown). Especially if the students have never heard of a conch, this prop allows them to better "visualize" what the boys are experiencing on the island.

A particularly creative math teacher on our staff uses a large rawhide dog bone as a hall pass. He says one of his favorite props, though, is an overhead pointer shaped like a human hand with a pointing index finger.

I remember my high school drama teacher showing us a large, three dimensional model of The Globe Theater when we were studying Shakespearean scenes. We have the same model at our school, and our ninth-grade teachers show it to students when we do *Romeo and Juliet*.

Using props does not have to be a huge production. Objects close at hand can be used as effective props. Sometimes using a prop can be as simple as raising the very book from which you are teaching over your head in referring to the text, the way a preacher raises *The Bible* to refer to Scripture. In this case, it is the very simplicity which makes it such an exciting visual for your students and a powerful moment in the lesson.

Experiment with the use of props and costumes in your own classroom. Be as simple or elaborate as you wish. See what works and what falls flat on its face. Both costumes and props are easily and inexpensively obtained by browsing at local thrift stores, swap meets, or garage sales. You can also dig around your own house (or grandma's old clothes closet or grandpa's old tool shed or whatever) to find exactly the right prop to liven up your lesson. When you adjust props and costumes to fit your own personal teaching style, they can make each lesson a memorable and dramatic experience and give your performance style a sense of variety and depth.

29

IMAGINARY OBJECTS

One of the questions that has plagued teachers since the advent of the little red schoolhouse is: "How do I get all the supplies I need without paying for most of them myself?"

The answer to this, simply put, is: imaginary objects.

The concept of imaginary objects is often one of the first taught in beginning drama classes. Beginning actors, however, are not always as receptive to the idea of imaginary objects as drama teachers would hope.

"Why do we have to use imaginary objects?" one of my beginning year drama students typically pouted, "My dad has this really cool authentic sword from World War II, and I just *have* to use it in my scene."

"No, you don't," I'd say. "You have one right here." And with that, I'd brandish a huge (imaginary) sword I pulled from my scabbard and swing it in the direction of the student. Invariably, he'd duck as if I'd nearly decapitated him.

After a momentary pause to insure that all his limbs were intact, the student would mutter, "Oh," and slink back to his seat. Usually, that ended the argument on the effectiveness of imaginary objects.

The reason imaginary objects are taught first is simple. For the rest of the year, the students will always have, at his or her disposal, the materials necessary to be successful in the class. I explain to the novice thespians that if they use imaginary objects, and *believe* in them, the audience will believe in them, too, and have much more confidence in the story the actors are trying to tell. The audience will concentrate more on the message and less on whether or not the props are "real enough" for the performance.

Thornton Wilder used this concept effectively in his play *Our Town*. With an empty stage and only a handful of props, Wilder wove a universal story of family, memory, and regret—told primarily through the use of pantomime and imaginary objects. In successful productions of *Our Town*, the imaginary objects are used so faithfully and believably that the audience never doubts the reality of the situation.

Teachers also do not have to depend on elaborate costumes, props, and materials to sell their performance. They can, but they don't have to. They can use their judgment as to when to go and get "the real thing" and when to just pull it out of thin air.

With imaginary objects, everything you need is at your fingertips.

Using imaginary objects is beneficial whether you are teaching allegory in English or combustion in chemistry. In *Romeo and Juliet*, for example, there is a scene where Juliet is about to drink the potion she was given by Friar Lawrence. In another scene, Romeo is about to poison himself. In either case, you may wish you had a vial. In chemistry, you may also want a vial to use as a visual aid to show the reaction of two different chemicals when they are combined. Certainly you *could* find a real vial, but it really isn't necessary.

The objective in these two scenarios is to give the students a sense of the reality of the situation. You want them to conceive of what you're talking about. You want them to experience your message.

In short, you want the students to visualize the vial.

There are a number of ways to achieve this. Each teacher has an arsenal of supplies and activities and strategies that help him or her communicate his or her message: overheads, handouts, pictures, films, videos, audiotapes, guest speakers, group projects, etc. Teachers will use whatever it takes to enlighten their students or help them understand a concept. Few teachers, however, realize that imaginary objects are the least expensive and, in some cases, most effective of supplies. They are quite literally the easiest supplies to get your hands on.

Here's how to use an imaginary object:

Let's use the example of the vial. First, you must believe in the object. See it on the podium or desk. Visualize it. See its dimensions, color, size, and weight. The more detail you can give it in your mind's eye, the more real it will become for you. Walk over to it slowly to create suspense and anticipation in your students. Walk to it as if you see it. Your students will be intrigued, wondering what their teacher is doing. Pick it up using clear and delineated movements and tense your muscles to indicate the weight and bulk of the object (sloppy or unpunctuated movements or muscles not tensed in the *lifting* of the object will destroy the illusion).

Pick up the object from a surface (table, podium, desk, etc.). This enhances the reality of the object much more than if it appears out of nowhere. If a performer plucks an object from mid-air, the audience's question becomes "Where did he get that?" which immediately distracts the viewer from the reality of the performance. Similarly, when finished with an object, set it down. Don't just drop it or let it vanish into thin air simply letting it go. The illusion you've created will cause the viewer's mind to see the object falling to the ground and, once again, they will be more concerned with the fate of the object (Did it break? Roll down the aisle? What?) than with your performance.

When lifting an object, leave enough room in the opening of your hands and fingertips for the bulk of the vial. If you are Romeo or Juliet drinking from the vial, slowly offer it up to your mouth, close your eyes, and drink with passion, remembering to swallow to sell the moment as "real." Set the object down. Finally, wait a beat (the time it takes for the performance to reach and sink into the audience), then move on.

If you are doing the chemistry lesson mentioned earlier, envision the vial on the desk, walk to it, pick it up a second one, pour them one at a time into an imaginary bowl—being careful not to spill any, of course—and then *react* to whatever the result of the combination of those two chemicals would be (i.e., jump back if an explosion, smile at the change of color, wrinkle your nose and cough at the pungency of the gas, etc.).

The right imaginary object, and its effective use, will create a moment your students are not likely to forget.

Using imaginary objects takes an act of faith. You must have the confidence that you will be believable and that you will not look foolish. Ironically, not only will you *not* look foolish, but you will most likely create for your students a very "real" teachable moment. If you commit to the use of imaginary objects, you will be providing your students with a sense of the "magic" of learning.

My drama students learned about that magic the hard way. Many first year actors sign up for the Drama class figuring they will immediately be transformed into a herd of little Leonardo DiCaprios and Drew Barrymores and learn how to act using real props and costumes, not the phony "pretend" stuff I make them use. "That's for children," is the vibe I sensed every time I introduced the concept of imaginary objects. "I'm an actor!" they think, "not a five year-old playing house in the backyard." I always listened to their complaints patiently and took them in stride, while trying to think of the best way to convince them of the importance of this skill as part of the foundation of their acting technique.

In this case, however, it was another teacher who did the convincing. The next year I went to a school play directed by the advanced drama teacher. In a very beautifully directed and emotionally moving scene, the actors played migrant workers picking grapes in a large field. In film and television, of course, these same actors would surely be picking actual grapes in some actual farmer's actual field. Theater, however, is never afforded the luxury of "shooting on location."

This also accounts for much of its magic.

So there were my grumbling first year students—now "seasoned" actors and actresses—emoting their hearts out on the main stage, envisioning imaginary grapes, stretching and massaging pained back muscles that didn't really ache, and dropping their imaginary crop into their imaginary buckets in the middle of some imaginary field. In the end they learned, as we all do, through practice, empathy, and experience. It was a magic moment in the play *because* of the imaginary objects, not in spite of them.

The beauty of using imaginary objects is that whatever we need is sitting right in front of us—a sword, an apple, a baseball bat, a rowboat, whatever is needed to give your lessons depth, credibility, and a sense of imagination and wonder. It's all there for the taking. And with this technique, you never have to worry about saving receipts, rummaging through bargain racks at The Salvation Army, or being reimbursed by an anemic department budget.

Take advantage of imaginary objects.

Reach for what you need.

30

MUSIC AND SOUND

o o o o o o o o o o o o o o o o o o o o o o o o o o o o o o o o

"Extraordinary how potent cheap music is."

—Noel Coward
  Private Lives

Music is a powerful force. It entertains us, informs us, heals us. Music also affects us on levels of which we're not even always aware. Think about scary movies, for instance. The moment something really scary is about to happen, ominous music starts playing on the soundtrack. The first purpose of this is to inform us that something scary is, in fact, about to happen. But the other reason this happens is to get us in the mood and mindset to *be* scared. We are getting the same information ("be very scared") from two different channels (the image on the screen and the music on the soundtrack). The music echoes what we're seeing on the screen, reinforcing in us whatever the director wishes us to think or feel.

Music also affects our memory. Certain pieces of music become so popular they are instantly recognizable by the majority of "people-on-the-street." For example, most of us—if coerced—could hum the theme from *Star Wars*. Fans of show tunes would be more than happy to reenact the dirgeful opening chords of *Phantom of the Opera*. As a member of the television generation, I can probably hum more T.V. theme songs and commercial jingles than Ted Turner. In a nanosecond, I can make instant distinctions between the instrumental themes of *Bewitched, I Dream of Jeannie, and Bonanza*. These songs and tunes are such an ingrained part of our lives, they have become part of our cultural literacy.

Sound and music can be just as effective when used as tools to set mood in the classroom.

<u>Music</u>

Students enjoy music. There are as many uses for music in the classroom as there are individual lesson plans. The opportunities are truly endless. With a little imagination and effort, a teacher can find appropriate music to complement any concept, unit, or activity.

Most teachers I know use music in the classroom a number of times during the school year. English teachers use various songs to amplify themes in certain pieces of literature. As an introduction to *The Great Gatsby*, for instance, I asked our choir teacher for samples of music from the 20s, especially samples of jazz. He loaned me a Jelly Roll Morton CD, which I played for my juniors to show them the contemporary music of the time.

One of the themes of *Gatsby* concerns the blind pursuit of "The American Dream." I usually end the unit of this book by playing those same junior classes the song *Born to Run* by Bruce Springsteen. This song deals with the latter half of this century's disillusionment with this dream, especially by members of the working class (which contrasts nicely with the rich folk in *Gatsby*). Not only are the students listening to music in the classroom but, by studying the Boss's lyrics, they are being exposed to a kind of contemporary poetry as well.

Similarly, from the earliest periods of their lives, children are taught new concepts through the use of music. Consider, for example, the alphabet song. By associating the lyrics (the letters of the alphabet) with a catchy tune, children have an easier time learning their ABC's. In fact, I've seen adult office workers humming this little ditty as they file!

A student of mine recently brought in a CD of songs from ABC Television's series of educational short films called *Scholastic Rock*. I played these songs about grammar as we practiced fixing sentence fragments and run-ons. I listened to these songs when they appeared in little vignettes during Saturday morning cartoons when I was a child (the jazzy/bluesy Conjunction Junction, sung by former *Tonight Show* trumpeter Jack Sheldon, was always one of my favorites). The topics ranged from the multiplication tables (an extremely hip rabbit tells us how to multiply by seven) to civics lessons (again, Jack Sheldon portraying a rolled up piece of legislation on "I'm Just a Bill"). To this day, I cannot recite The Preamble to The Constitution of the United States unless I sing it to the tune the *Scholastic Rock* people put it to.

Mr. Morrissey, my high school Spanish teacher, taught us vocabulary by playing Spanish songs on an ancient, school district-issue phonograph. He told us one day in 1979, "Class, we're going to learn some songs this year by a man named Julio Iglesias. I know you've never heard of him, but he's a very famous singer in the countries where Spanish is spoken." This is just further evidence that Mr. Morrissey was a fine teacher and ahead of his time. In less than five years, Mr. Iglesias was a household name in the U.S., as well. Mr. Morrissey understood that music would help us retain the vocabulary words, which we could then use in contexts other than one of Julio's romantic ballads.

A social studies teacher I know makes her unit on the 60's infinitely more relevant and immediate for her students by playing songs of the era, specifically teaching what amounts to a mini-unit on Bob Dylan. If my high school history teacher had *ever* played any Dylan, I would have clutched my heart and fallen out of my chair on the spot. This same teacher also uses Billy Joel's "We Didn't Start the Fire" to teach the litany of historical events found in that song.

A science teacher at our school uses music and choreography to teach the parts of the heart and how they function. Called, "The Heart Disco," this music and movement piece he developed includes dancing, singing, miming, imaginary objects, and rhythm. Recently, he used music again during a unit on microbes. During our recent 50's dress-up day, he was not Elvis, but "Elvirus." He rewrote many of The King's most popular songs to include references to his material on microbes ("You ain't nuthin' but a paramecium, multiplyin' all the time"). One of our career and family studies teachers uses "Keep Your Hands to Yourself" by The Georgia Satellites during her discussion on abstinence.

Music can also serve as accompaniment to other forms of literature. One of my favorite spoken word CDs is of Jack Kerouac reading his poetry with completely improvised piano accompaniment by Steve Allen. Kerouac knew something that good literature teachers know. In general, music is an excellent addition to any unit on poetry. Playing instrumental or classical music behind a poetry reading or recitation gives it a dramatic, performance-style feeling. Given the right props, costumes, and environment, you can even recreate a beat generation, coffeehouse, open-mike-kind-of-experience right in your classroom.

Jack would be proud.

Although I am not one of them, there are also those who are talented enough to play their own instruments in class, sing, and/or bring music to their students through the immediacy of live performance. Teachers can also rely on talented students to play and sing in classroom projects and assignment. During a recent unit on Native American literature, for example, some students of mine wrote and performed original songs that were relevant to the themes we were studying and members of the choir even came over one day and sang some Native American songs for those classes.

While there is no end to the number of ways music can be used effectively in the classroom, other types of sound can be used as well.

Sound

The use of sound in the classroom can be an unusual and exciting addition to any teaching performance style. A teacher's creativity in using sound can lead to some wonderful experiences for the students. Using sound effectively in the classroom can be as simple as pounding the podium or desk or hitting the board with a pointer to emphasize or echo something that is being discussed. For instance, when reading literature to my classes, I pound on my podium or desk as I read to underscore scenes where there is thunder, yelling, cannon fire, and/or other loud or pounding sounds. Opportunities for percussion during a lesson plan are hidden moments of drama. Imagine, for example, what the creative teacher could do with a cheap set of garage sale bongo drums.

Another, more technical use of sound has become available to the classroom teachers with the advent of books on tape. While many English teachers initially cringe at the thought of students NOT reading a book, I find these tapes very helpful. They help my students create the "movie" of the book in their minds and provide a storytelling experience in the classroom. While I advise against using them *instead* of a book, they can complement a book nicely, especially for reluctant readers.

Many times my students will open their books and follow along as a professional actor reads the story with, of course, great diction, inflection, and distinctive character voices. In some cases, the authors read their own works. I have used audiotaped versions of *Of Mice and Men, Animal Farm, The Crucible, and Lord of the Flies.* As empirical research bears out, when students receive material through more than one channel, there is a greater likelihood they will walk away having retained more of the important concepts.

How effective books on tape can be when used in class became very clear to me a few years when I taught *Pigs in Heaven,* by Barbara Kingsolver, for the first time. This book is written by a woman and has female protagonists, so the tone and rhythm of the novel is wildly different than *The Catcher in the Rye,* which we had just finished. I opened my *Catcher* unit by reading the first chapter aloud to my classes. Holden Caulfield's voice is so distinctive and conversational, that reading the beginning usually sets his voice in my students' heads and serves them well for the rest of the book. They seem then to better understand his sentence patterns and the rhythm of his speech. I did the same thing for *Pigs*, however, and at the end of the unit several students said, "I really enjoyed the book, but I couldn't get your Holden Caulfield voice out of my head."

The following year I opened my *Pigs in Heaven* unit with the audio-taped version, read by Barbara Kingsolver herself. Their understanding of the main character's voice, both literally and figuratively, was much improved. I suppose it also helped that the words were being said by the very person who *created* the main characters. They were able to understand Kingsolver's personal writing style better and could also more easily follow what the protagonists were experiencing without the "maleness" of my voice interfering or causing them unnecessary "static."

The use of music and sound to underscore, amplify, and extend concepts or ideas that are relevant to the material can be an extremely effective performance technique. Just as the ominous music in the scary movie has us warning the main character not to go into the basement with the baseball bat, music and sound can invite our students to go places they pretend not to want to go for fear they are too scary, but which they secretly wish to visit, anyway.

31

LIGHTING

When it comes to lighting, classroom teachers probably think they have two choices: on or off. While this is true, in theory, an inventive teacher can not only make wise use of both "on" and "off," but can also devise lighting alternatives which will keep their students engaged in the lesson, as well as guessing what the teacher might come up with next. Certainly no one expects teachers to create laser light or special effects shows worthy of a KISS concert, but there are specific and worthwhile things you can do with lighting in the classroom to make your lessons more dramatic and to help create an appropriate mood for them.

In every classroom across America, teachers subconsciously make lighting choices every day. Some teachers, for instance, choose to leave window blinds opened or closed. There are advantages and disadvantages to each. I tend to leave mine closed because, otherwise, I've noticed students become quite distracted by good weather or when their friends come strolling down the hallway. Invariably, one of these chuckleheads finds it necessary to wave to his friends in my class or, worse, place his cupped hands (it's usually a boy) on my window and peer in as if it were a 42nd Street Peep Show.

What I miss out on with this choice, however, is the great benefits of natural light which can increase productivity as well as the positive feelings in the classroom, putting everyone in a better mood.

There are any number of times teachers make specific lighting choices to complement their subject matter, regardless of how basic their lighting equipment. During one section of *The Adventures of Huckleberry Finn*, for example, I make a lighting choice as I read out loud to my students. First, I turn off my lights and have my students close their eyes or put their heads on their desk. Next, I read a section where Huck describes watching a sunrise and I ask my students to play the "movie" in their minds and see in their mind's eye what Huck is seeing as the sun comes up over the Mississippi River. As I get to the end of the section, I turn the lights on a bank at a time (I have two switches—one for each bank of lights in my room). While admittedly a basic maneuver, it is my hope that this lighting choice in some way reminds them of a sunrise and aids in their ability to visualize the scene as well as somewhat echoing the lighting Huck experiences in that scene. Even if my classroom were equipped with an inexpensive dimmer switch, this activity would increase in its effectiveness.

Earlier, I mentioned my seventh grade teacher who recited Poe's "The Tell-Tale Heart" in a dark room using only a candle. While using proper care and obtaining proper permission, of course, candles can be an excellent source of light and do, naturally, set a mood for whatever will be taking place. There are any number of books, units, or concepts where candles could be used as a lighting choice to enhance the material being covered. Having candle flames flickering when students enter the room increases anticipation and wonder, creating young minds that are eager to listen and learn. Also, lighting a candle at just the right moment in a lecture, speech, or monologue can also be a very dramatic, and unforgettable image.

A teacher with an imagination can also use special kinds or types of lights to change the mood in the classroom. A science teacher I know recently mentioned using spotlights, blacklights, strobelights, and Christmas-style lights in his classroom at various times and for various lessons. His ingenuity and imagination regarding lighting has clearly been paying off for him. His classroom has no longer relied on an "on" and "off" mentality, and has certainly taken on a personality different from any other classroom on campus. Students experience his classroom, therefore, in a more unique way than any other classroom they visit during the course of their school day. Another teacher I know has several living-room-style lamps set around the classroom which lends the classroom a decidedly "homey" feel.

Even the use of something as simple as a flashlight in a dark room can be effective. When pointed out at the class, on a wall, or at a certain bit of information on a chalkboard, a flashlight can "pinpoint" important aspects of a lesson. When pointed up at one's own face, a spooky and mysterious "skull-like" image is created and can be used to change the atmosphere and chemistry in the room. This effect is perfect for Halloween units, more Poe stories, or "mysteries" of any kind in any subject matter.

Just as your students have more setting than "on" and "off," your choices in regard to classroom lighting can operate on just as expansive a spectrum, and you can "paint" your lessons with as colorful and varied a palette.

32

MULTI-MEDIA

In terms of multi-media technology in the classroom, we've certainly come along way since those days in elementary school where we were thrilled to be watching 16mm films on those old projectors where the film burned like marshmallows over a campfire and whose bulbs always seemed to give up the ghost at the most climactic point in the movie. Even more ancient were those filmstrip machines where the teacher put the soundtrack album on the phonograph and a ringing bell or chime signaled when to stop reading the caption and switch the picture being projected on the screen. The filmstrip is to the classroom as a chisel and stone is to the word-processor I'm using to crank out this last chapter.

As we entered the new millennium, however, almost every teacher in America has probably had some experience in the classroom with a video camera, VCR, tape recorder, or computer. We have yet to reach our potential, though, for how this equipment can improve our performance skills in the classroom. Below are some ideas on how to use multi-media equipment to enhance the production value of our lesson.

Video Cameras

The first time I saw a videotape-recording machine was in my very first drama class. Mrs. Myers, our drama teacher, informed us that she was going to be recording our most recent scenes so we could watch them as she critiqued our performances. I was thrilled. For the first time in my life, I would be seeing myself on television. This was 1977, after all, when not all of us were used to seeing images of ourselves dancing around inside that little box in our living rooms. I'll never forget when she wheeled out the A/V cart. It was a beast. Spielberg could have used it as an extra in *Jurassic Park*. On the bottom level of the cart sat a giant box the size of a suitcase. This was the black and white reel-to-reel video tape recorder. A television was mounted on the top of the cart, to be used as the video monitor. Across from the tiny stage, Mrs. Myers had stationed a giant, tube-driven video camera that she would sit behind while she videotaped our scenes. The cassette style videotapes and color technology we enjoy today (not to mention palm-held video cameras or digital video images and editing) would not be perfected for classroom use for another twenty years or more!

The next day, we sat mesmerized as we watched our scenes as they glowed back at us in glorious monochrome. But even so, the use of that machinery enhanced Mrs. Myers's lesson and made it a moment from my education I cherish to this day.

Video cameras are woefully underused as tools of student instruction and teacher performance in the average classroom. The more inspired teachers I know use them regularly to capture oral presentations and group projects. The truly creative teachers, however, go the extra distance and use them for creating student-generated commercials, parodies, satires, video projects, role-plays, and lip synchs to songs. Imagine the learning potential of a commercial parody about selling Manhattan for $24 using a used car salesman routine or a lip synch to a 1920's jazz song or an original *Romeo and Juliet* rap song.

A group of teachers in my English Department teach the play *Antigone* and used to do a unit on moral dilemma and require their students to do a video project where they videotaped a scenario that included a modern day moral dilemma and resolution. The students formed groups and wrote/structured the scene themselves and played all the roles. It was always one of the most popular and talked about units (by teachers *and* students) that they did all year.

Coaches of sports teams have long understood the value of using videocameras. They tape their athletes' performances and use the tape to critique technique the same way Mrs. Myers used our tape to critique our performances. Baseball coaches, for instance, use video to improve a batter's stance; diving coaches use video to improve a diver's posture or her form in the air; and football coaches, naturally have had their teams reviewing game films since cavemen started bouncing coconuts off each others' heads.

Among multi-media choices available to the teacher, videotape is also the great equalizer. Using videotape is an effective method for teachers to offer suggestions to students without being critical. Feelings aren't hurt as readily because student and teacher are looking at the same piece of objective evidence—the videotape.

A college drama teacher of mine who used video extensively to coach his student actors suggested that videotape takes away all denial. Every year he would tell certain students about flaws in their acting technique and they would argue that they weren't making the errors he said they were making. After viewing the tape, they had no choice but to exclaim, "Gee, I guess I really do that, don't I?"

The use of video in the classroom is also becoming increasingly important as the educational theory pendulum swings toward the significance of senior projects and graduation exhibitions. As these activities gain clout, learning to give a creative, intelligent, and entertaining presentation is becoming more critical. Even in today's workforce, where the traditional autocratic boss is being replaced by Total Quality Management philosophies or The Work Team mentality, standing in front of a group of people and giving a confident and coherent address can set one apart from the masses. More than ever, employees are required to make effective and entertaining presentations about new ideas, products, or solutions to problems. The ability to record and review classroom presentations is an invaluable method of sharpening a student's presentation skills.

Other valuable uses of the video camera in the classroom include: capturing role-playing or improvised scenes on tape, mock job interviews, and—probably one of the most neglected uses of video cameras in the classroom: self-evaluation.

Teacher self-evaluation with a video camera is a practical activity for improvement and can eliminate a number of problems before your administrator comes in to perform the official evaluation. Video self-evaluation can be done easily and discreetly. On a day when you know you have an interesting lesson you wish to improve or simply monitor, merely place a video camera on a back table, bookshelf, window ledge, or perhaps, a tripod in an office doorway, and hit "record" before you begin. This is one time where the students' familiarity with video will work to your advantage because even if they become aware of the camera, they will lose interest eventually and will quickly go back to being themselves. After the lesson, you will have a valuable record of your performance that you can admire, revile, or critique as you wish.

As video technology expands, and its applications flourish in the educational arena, the use of video production will grow as well. Most larger high schools, and many smaller ones, now have access to video editing equipment that will turn their class projects into professional-style video segments that look like they came off the local television station.

Our school, for example, is quite new and our founders foresaw the video revolution and, therefore, included a state-of-the-art video production facility in the design of our school. This facility houses our telecommunication classes which produce, among other things, our daily bulletin and a weekly newsmagazine. These shows are then broadcast over our closed circuit television system to each and every classroom on campus. As lucky as our school is to have such a facility, one day programs like this will be commonplace in modern American schools.

Whether it's a gymnastic coach trying to tighten up a young gymnast's dismount, a History teacher recording a mock trial to make certain points about our justice system, or a group of students doing an improv about The Salem Witch Trials as a project for *The Crucible*, videotape not only improves a teacher's lesson, but provides a more accessible method of insight for the student.

Audio tape recorders and CD players

For a long time, the biggest technological advancement in the classroom came when we switched from using a record player during those filmstrips to using audio cassette recorder (thank goodness we were spared, as a profession, from the horror of the 8-track!). After the big switch in filmstrips, though, the use of tape recorders as a teaching tool grew more and more widespread until there were story listening stations, foreign language drills, and books on tape.

While still not as ubiquitous as video cameras, tape recorders can be an effective tool in creating an engaging lesson for your students. Students can record pre-written or original scripts (memorized, improvised, or reader's theater-style), do radio shows or plays, perform presentations, or record their own essays, poetry, or short stories.

There are a number of ways that the teacher can use a tape recorder or CD player as well. At the very least, classical or instrumental music played during silent seat work can increase the chances of focusing students and giving depth to their individual work, especially if the work is creative or imaginative. If the project is more active, you can experiment with rock music (be careful, though, given the subject matter of many of today's songs—keep song lyrics "classroom" appropriate).

If a story, speech, or passage needs to be read to a number of classes, for example, a teacher can tape it first and save wear and tear on the vocal chords. During the holidays, appropriate music can be played in the background to give depth to a reading, lecture, or other lesson. Imagine the fun of reading a Halloween story in class while using one of the many sound effects tapes available to create a spooky soundtrack.

Recently, the popularity and availability of CD "burners" has also increased. This cutting edge technology allows you to "write" on a CD, similar to the way we record on an audiotape recorder or VCR. Students of mine who have already purchased their own "burners" have recorded original music for projects, copied photographs for display on computer screens, and manipulated and edited digital video. I'm aware here that the moment this book is published most of the information I provide regarding the "newest" technology will be hopelessly outdated. *C'est La Vie.*

Most of these maneuvers only take an average-sized tape recorder or CD player (either a "boombox" or the CD/DVD drive on your computer) and not only sharpen a teacher's performance skills, but increase the teacher's chances of presenting a creative and theatrical, but still substantive, lesson.

Graphic Images

I remember high school assemblies where a professional company would compile a slide show of pictures taken on campus the previous semester and then time their appearance to songs that were currently popular. They had the technology to include wipes, blends, and fades between slides. The student body would gather in the auditorium, and we would watch ourselves on the giant screen and smile and laugh as our peers mugged to the tunes of Boston, Kansas, and Foreigner. The boys whooped and the girls squealed when they saw themselves and their friends sitting in the grass (with the ever present Martian antennae "V" placed behind your best friend's head, of course) or in line at the cafeteria looking frustrated because the line was moving slowly and they might run out of Nacho Cheese Doritos. It was exciting for all of us, but for me—the budding drama student—it was decidedly theatrical.

Though quaint in today's world of computer-generated images and animation, slides are still an effective way to touch student imagination. My tenth grade English teacher showed us a series of slides once and played background music (today we would call it "new age") and asked us to record our impressions, which we later used as material for our original short stories. I copied that assignment during my own student teaching assignment. The music doesn't have to be as finely timed as the professional production during our assemblies, just turn on some music and switch the slides in rhythm to the music. This is an excellent method for introducing students to topic, generating writing assignments, or bringing closure to a unit.

While slides take a little preparation and a few pieces of equipment, don't underestimate the power of a slide presentation and don't assume that slides are not "modern" enough. The same science teacher who requests free video ads, also has over 4,000 slides that he has taken over the years on a variety of science topics, including over 500 which show him reading his biology textbook in unusual places (a racing car, the Tour de France, Mount Whitney, etc.). This same teacher uses the Hyperstudio computer program which allows him to show a series of images synchronized with text (a film strip for the 21st Century, I suppose).

PowerPoint is another computer program that brings overhead and "slide show"-style presentations into the 21st Century. This program offers the teacher a plethora of template and structure options that make the organization of the presentation not only painless, but virtually foolproof. This software contains layouts, backgrounds, type styles, clip art, motion, and color. Sound and video clips can even be imported to enhance the project. Once finished, these presentations can either be printed as transparent overheads or, if the technology exists at your site, the presentation can be shown on a movie screen or white board. With the proper cables, your project can even be viewed on a television monitor.

Much like word-processing, PowerPoint creations can be saved in the computer to be used again year after year, eliminating the need to recreate them time after time. Imagine using PowerPoint in a history class to create a multi-media slide show on The 60's; envision how it would make the music, language, and political figures of that era come alive for students. Similarly, using it to outline the rules and regulations of Basketball in a Physical Education class, for example, would liven up what might potentially be a very dry and uninteresting section of the class. PowerPoint is a wonderfully logical and user-friendly program and with even a little effort, even the least computer-literate person on the staff can create whiz-bang presentations that will "wow" any audience.

A word of warning, though, it is easy to overdo the use of graphic images in the classroom.

Case in point: I received my Master's Degree from National University, a school which, for some reason, is big on requiring oral presentations. As several of us were pursuing the same degree, we saw each other in almost every class. Shelly, a technology mentor for her district, always brought the latest in video/computer/presentation equipment to use for her presentations. Her production values were stunning. She projected her monitor image onto the movie screen, she synchronized music to her computer images, and she ran video clips of her principal—with sound—through her computer. I was so impressed with this last bit of technology that the first time I saw it, I knew how moviegoers felt the first time they heard Al Jolson singing, "Mamee."

There were, however, two potential problems with Kelly's approach. The first was technical. Of the four or five presentations I saw Kelly give, at least two were hamstringed by technical difficulties "beyond her control." Machines weren't hooked up right (the number and complexity of connections, plugs, and cables was amazing—that anything worked *at all* is what surprised me), bulbs went out, plugs were pulled, or she experienced a myriad of other problems which completely paralyzed her performance. Nothing, of course, will lose your students' interest faster than a teacher who spends fifteen minutes saying, "Wait a minute. I think that's it. Yeah, I think I've got it. Hold on. Wait."

I've seen students lose interest in the time it takes to rewind a videotape.

Kelly's second problem was overkill. No doubt about it, her graphics were magical. She had us sitting, wide-eyed and gap-mouthed—like cavepeople staring at the advent of fire—but it is precisely because of her dazzling special effects that I cannot tell you the topic of a single one of her presentations. She had so much going on, her images were so overwhelming (or sometimes just plain "busy") that her medium became more important than her message.

We are a generation, like it or not, that was raised on the video image. As a society, we respond to the visuals and get some of our most significant cultural images from movies, television, home video, and—for better or worse—MTV. As some people see it, teachers have two basic choices: we can be conservative and traditional and pooh-pooh the advent of computers, video, and other forms of technology in the classroom. Or we can embrace the new technology and outfit our classrooms with all of the state-of-the-art equipment we can get our hands on because, as the experts tell us, this new generation will learn better because they are already more adept at these machines than are we.

A more realistic approach lies somewhere in between. As the pendulum of educational fads tends to swing in extreme arcs, so do teachers' approaches to those new fads. In this case, many teachers innocently wanting to welcome the new advances fill their classrooms with all these new toys and allow them to run their students, their curriculums, and their professional lives.

As teachers, we need to be aware of the new options available to us and be "up" on their applications in the classroom, but they are merely tools of the trade and we should neither shun them nor allow them to replace our personal interaction with our students.

Video, audio, slides, and computer-generated images and animation are all used in the modern theater to communicate a message to the audience.

Can we afford to do less in the classroom?

33

CURTAIN CALL

When you are ready to rehearse a balanced combination of the techniques outlined in this book, and then commit to implementing them into your regular curriculum and teaching style, your "stage presence" in the classroom will improve exponentially.

The key is to keep reading, working, and practicing.

There are two more concepts that you should know in order to prepare a performance approach each and every time you step into the classroom. These two concepts are: Know Your Audience and Know Your Limits.

Know Your Audience

Let's say I am a professional stand-up comedian. This means it is my job to perform in front of people and entertain them for an hour or so—in a humorous fashion, preferably. I may be required to perform in a number of venues for a number of different audiences. Audiences, by definition, subscribe to the snowflake theory—no two are alike. Each group of people will have its own collective personality, its own chemistry. As a comedian, I understand that different crowds respond to different kinds of material.

If I am performing for a large crowd in a banquet hall for a formal dinner for some high profile charity, for instance, I would not necessarily tell the same kinds of jokes than if I were performing in the smoky bowling alley lounge on the outskirts of town by the Interstate.

Although there will always be some overlap, these two crowds—generally speaking—bring different backgrounds, experiences, and value systems to my performance. As a performer, I must be sensitive to this. I need to know what will please them (as well as displease them). I need to know "where they're coming from" as an audience.

In short, I must know my audience.

As teachers, we face the same responsibility to understand our audiences. We must be sensitive to each group's personal make-up and its individual personality. We need to know which material will play and which material will crash and burn. This is not as easy as it sounds. Some comedians erroneously assume the formal dinner audience will only laugh at high brow jokes and that, of course, the smoky lounge group who is straining to hear me over the strike on lane 13 will always want it down and dirty. Teachers, too, will misread their audiences on occasion and, just when they think they have the audience chemistry pegged, they will be forced to shift their paradigm. Fortunately for teachers, it is this challenge which also keeps our jobs interesting and spontaneous.

Teachers must know which classes will respond to being treated as intellectuals and which groups appreciate a more informal, practical, down-to-earth, and less "high-brow" approach. We must discern which of our audiences can handle "adult" concepts, examples, and remarks, and which audience will require us to keep it on a more elementary level. Costumes, music, and character voices may work for one of your more dramatic classes, while energy, projection, and inflection may be more effective in one of your classes with more auditory learners.

On more than one occasion I have witnessed a teacher who did not understand the audience with which he or she was dealing. This instructor went on to present material that either caused him or herself embarrassment, shame, or in some extreme cases, censure.

Teachers cannot be petrified of pushing things too far or offending their audience, however. Furthermore, you sometimes have to go too far to know what's enough. Teachers must learn where the line is with each of their classes; and it will be different with each class, each year.

Know Your Limits

When performing in the classroom, it is critical that we recognize our own personal levels of comfort. Everyone has limits. There are things we are secure doing and saying in front of our classes and things we wouldn't do even if we were told desperate criminals were holding our immediate family hostage in an abandoned mine shaft.

It is important to listen to these limits because students do not like to see teachers who are uncomfortable with *how* they're presenting anymore than they like to see teachers who are uncomfortable with *what* they are presenting. What this means is that if you feel silly wearing costumes or speaking character voices, then don't. It may take some time for you to build up a confidence that allows you to experiment with these techniques. For now, maybe your focus should be pacing, structure, and relaxation.

If you are reading this book, you are at least somewhat interested in improving your "stage presence" in the classroom. Some teachers, though, are more reserved and conservative. Still others are afraid that certain performance-oriented techniques will make them lose their sense of professional dignity or "distance" in front of their students. My advice to those teachers is to listen to their comfort level and only implement those techniques which work for them personally.

Teachers who are comfortable with their teaching and performing style have a much better chance of effectively communicating a message to their audience. Arguably, they also have a better time in the classroom themselves which may encourage them to stay in that classroom longer. An uncomfortable teacher, on the other hand, is likely to be so self-conscious that valuable material will avoided, skimmed over, or simply left out. Do yourself a favor and take a personal inventory of your performing technique comfort levels *before attempting anything described in this book.*

I have always made every attempt in my own teaching style to know my audiences and know my limits. It has made many decisions infinitely easier. I keep these two concepts in mind when planning a lesson, especially when it contains the performance elements mentioned in this book. These two concepts guide each of my performance choices, regardless of grade level or subject area. They make my job easier, because if I understand my audience and recognize my own personal limits, certain choices become obvious and others become clearly inappropriate. Know Your Audience and Know Your Limits are two precepts which have basically become second nature in my lesson planning and my classroom management. They are the mission statement of my own personal philosophy of performance in the classroom. When integrated into our daily approach to performing in the classroom, these approaches give a structure to our overall performance technique.

Finally, I hope that using some or all of the acting techniques in this book helps improve your stage presence in the classroom. It has for me and, while stage presence is only one of the many balls a modern educator is expected to juggle, using these techniques has made me a more effective teacher overall. I hope you find the same true for you—after some good old-fashioned rehearsal, of course!

Good luck and good performing.

About the Author

photo by John Goodman

Daniel Tricarico received his teaching credential in 1987 and earned his Master's Degree in Educational Administration in 1997. His professional acting experience culminated in appearances on *General Hospital* and *The Bold and the Beautiful*. Currently he works as a high school English teacher in San Diego, California, where he lives with his wife and two daughters.

0-595-23402-X